From
Orphans
To
Children

Discovering The Heart of a Father

CLAUDIA GALVÁN GIL

For other materials and resources, visit us at:
GuipilBooks.com

© 2023 by Claudia Galván Gil
All rights reserved "From Orphans to Children"
Originally published in Spanish by Editorial Guipil "De Huérfanos a Hijos"

Published by **Editorial Güipil**
Miami, FL - Winston-Salem, NC. United States of America

All rights reserved. No portion or part of this work may be reproduced, stored in an information retrieval system, or transmitted in any form or by any means (electronic, mechanical, photocopying, recording, etc.) without the prior permission of the publishers, except for brief quotations and reviews.

This publication contains the opinions and ideas of its author. Its purpose is to provide informative and useful material on the topics discussed in the publication. It is sold with the understanding that the author and the publisher are not engaged in rendering financial, health, or any other kind of personal and professional services in the book. The reader should consult his or her personal advisor or other competent professional before adopting any of the suggestions in this book or drawing deductions from it. The author and the publisher expressly disclaim all responsibility for any effect, loss, or risk, personal or otherwise, incurred as a consequence, directly or indirectly, of the use and application of any of the contents of this book.

Bible verses indicated with NVI have been taken from the Holy Bible, New International Version, NVI. ©1999 by Biblica, Inc. Used by permission of Zondervan. All rights reserved worldwide. www.zonderban.com.

Bible verses indicated with RV60 have been taken from the Holy Bible, Reina Valera 1960 version. ©1960 Sociedades Bíblicas en América Latina; ©renovado 1988 Sociedades Bíblicas Unidas. Used with permission. Reina Valera 1960© is a registered trademark of the American Bible Society.

Bible verses indicated with NTV have been taken from the Holy Bible, New Living Translation,
© Tyndale House Foundation 2008, 2009, 2010. Used by permission of Tyndale House Publishers, Inc., 351 Executive Dr., Carol Stream, IL 60188, United States of America. All rights reserved.

Güipil Publishing House

Editorial Güipil. First edition 2023
ISBN: 978-1-953689-67-2
EditorialGuipil.com
Category: Practical Life / Family / Inspiration

To the Heavenly Father, who has allowed me to write my story, which testifies of His grace and faithfulness. To Jesus, for His immense love for humanity. To my children, Daniela, Joshua, Gabriel, and Genesis. To you, dear reader, who are seeking to know more about God within these pages.

Acknowledgments

I thank the Heavenly Father for the life of my husband, who has supported me greatly in this project.

Mario, thank you for loving me all these years and for always being present for our children.

I thank my mother for not giving up and not surrendering to adversity. I admire her faith, courage, and determination.

I thank my sister María José and every member of our family. My sister has been a gift from God in my life.

Also, my pastors Carlos and Stephanie Ferreyro for their teachings, prayers, and advice.

I thank Rebeca Segebre and her entire team at Editorial Güipil for giving me the opportunity to publish this book. Thank you for all the academic preparation, support, and motivation to continue writing.

Table of Contents

Acknowledgments

Chapter 1
Discovering The Heart of a Father 9

Chapter 2
The Wound of Rejection 21

Chapter 3
Parenting Styles 33

Chapter 4
A Journey into the Unknown 51

Chapter 5
Identity 69

Chapter 6
A Father After God's Own Heart 93

Chapter 7
Healing, a Gift from the Father 119

Epilogue
From Orphan to Daughter 147

About the Author 151

Bibliography 153

CHAPTER 1
DISCOVERING THE HEART OF A FATHER

In the course of my work as a counselor, I've had the privilege of connecting with numerous individuals who, like me, have navigated the complexities of growing up in dysfunctional families. As I embarked on my own healing journey, I discovered a profound truth: to truly comprehend how our past shapes our present, we must delve into our personal histories. It is through this introspection that we can acknowledge the significance of every experience, recognizing that each moment has played a role in propelling us towards the future that God has lovingly prepared.

In this book, I will present you with tools to aid in the healing of emotional traumas and the wounds of rejection and abandonment. Additionally, I will provide exercises to help you uncover your identity and purpose in accordance with God's plan for your life. Through these pages, You will discover the wonder that is God's presence in every aspect of our lives.

To truly convey the message of this book, It is necessary for me to share glimpses of my own childhood and the experiences I endured. By doing so, you will comprehend how these experiences shaped me and how these experiences shaped the different stages of my life. Perhaps you will find yourself identifying with some of my own encounters and discover how you, too, have managed to survive situations that were meant to defeat you, but instead have only strengthened you and propelled you forward.

My mother told me that when she was about to give birth, my father had disengaged himself from the responsibility of his role, and she had to go through the pregnancy alone. My father never spoke about that matter; the only thing he would say is that he was overjoyed when I was born. He arrived at Lenin Fonseca Hospital in Managua with a yellow baby basket, as he had hoped for a boy; A fact that I did not like to hear because it made me think that perhaps his joy vanished when he realized I was a girl.

Many years later, while taking care of my ailing father, he said to me:

"You are my continuation, and all I can advise and tell you is: live. Time is like life for those who waste it."

My father possessed a genuine passion for writing and a profound admiration for philosophy and poetry. Every now and then, he would engage in conversations that carried a philosophical flair. In all the time we spent together, he never unveiled the struggles he and my mother endured, nor did he utter a single negative word about her, even when certain members of her family would speak ill of him.

I didn't spend much time with my father in my early years, but the moments I did share with him left a lasting impression on my memory and heart. I never understood why he didn't oppose my mother and my grandmother, who made decisions without considering what he wanted to do. Today, I can see that perhaps the guilt of what happened before I was born made him believe that he had lost all authority over decisions that involved my well-being. I can also say now that my father was distant from God, he did not know Him and did not seek Him, which made it impossible to establish a family; God initially intended and led us to a life where each of us would know our identity, our purpose, and above all, His love. It is impossible to love others if we are not first filled with His love.

MY EARLIEST MEMORIES WITH MY GRANDMOTHERS

Both of my grandmothers would tell me stories about my parents' childhood and how well they performed in school. My father was born in Pueblo Nuevo and grew up in the city of Estelí, in northern Nicaragua, while my mother was born and raised in the western city of León, also known as the University City. Both of them had moved to the capital at a young age: my father to study accounting, finance, and law. He managed to graduate with a doctoral degree in law and practiced as a lawyer for forty years.

My mother had come to Managua in search of work and a better life. She always had a talent for hairstyling and cosmetology, something she learned through great sacrifice. My mother arrived in the city alone, without knowing anyone, but God opened doors and opportunities for her. He also removed people from her path who tried to take advantage of her youth and lack of experience.

My father enjoyed taking care of himself, and he met my mother at a spa while he was getting a manicure; he was intrigued by her, and eventually introduced her to his family; however, my Mom told me that my paternal grandmother never accepted her. I believe that when mothers decide to meddle in the lives of their adult children, it is the grandchildren who suffer the consequences. It is crucial to understand that we should honor our parents, but we are also called to become one flesh with the person we marry before God and mankind. Later on, I will share more about the matriarchy that shaped my family across generations, where the voices of the men were silenced and overshadowed.

I was born in 1981, two years after the defeat of Anastasio Somoza Debayle and the advancement of the Sandinista National Liberation Front, better known as the FSLN in Nicaragua. Despite the political climate and the dysfunction within the family nucleus, I remember being a very active, mischievous child who was always happily playing outside.

My grandmother, with whom I spent most of my childhood, had fruit trees and a huge backyard. She loved cooking and made delicious dishes to sell and generate income. She also sewed using an old sewing machine; "Singer" was one of the first words I learned to read. She used that machine to make my first dresses and the first pink backpack I took to kindergarten. My grandmother was the embodiment of unrelenting determination and hardwork.

Growing up in post-revolutionary Nicaragua, our lives were marked by periods of uncertainty and upheaval. Amidst these trying times, my parents would make occasional visits, with my mother bringing along essential supplies. I remember standing in long lines with my grandmother to receive what the ration card indicated or whatever we could manage to find. Thankfully, Nicaragua is an agricultural country, and we could easily buy food from the local markets in León. My uncle, who was in the Sandinista army after being recruited at the age of fifteen, would bring back peaches in syrup from the port of Corinto, Chinandega. I remember them vividly because they are still one of my favorite desserts. León has always been a vibrant city with activities happening all around.

My mother's siblings made every effort to take care of my grandmother and me. My mother's eldest brother would pick us up on Sundays and take us to the cathedral, also known as the Central Park, where he would buy me a bag of jocotes, a type of plum, which I would eat with salt and lime. And, without fail, he always had a bag of toasted bread in hand, ready to be shared with the pigeons that frequented the park. I had always loved birds, although at that time I didn't know that God was using me to provide them with food. I would spend those afternoons in great joy, finding ways to climb the majestic lions in front of the Cathedral; That was until it was time to return home and I realized along the way that I was always the child without her parents. No one said anything to me; on the contrary, they included me in many activities. But at the age of five, I started to notice that my reality was different from that of other children. The Mother's Day celebrations didn't help either, as my grandmother would always attend to receive the red carnation we had made in class.

In Nicaragua, the word "mota" was widely used at that time because many children had lost their parents in the war. It means orphan. When I started the first grade, my parents enrolled me in one of the best schools in León. At the Calasanz School, there was a particular girl who used to bother me when I was six years old. She would say to me,

"You're a 'mota'." I didn't know what that word meant, but the other children would laugh, point at me, and keep their distance.

One day, after school, I waited for this girl and confronted her. Unfortunately, things didn't end well, as one of the teachers sent me to pray in front of a crucifix and repent for something I didn't understand. Sitting before the crucified Christ stayed in my mind for a long time; I remember the fear I felt seeing Him bloody and nailed to the cross. I don't recall anyone taking the time to explain to me why He was like that. I started asking many questions and wanted to know more about God.

One weekend, we were invited to a Christian vigil. My grandmother's cooking was very popular, and the evangelicals, as they were called in the neighborhood, were good at organizing their activities. Even in times of scarcity, God always provided and we were warmly greeted as if we had known each other for a long time. During those days, we were on hurricane alert, and the group came together in prayer for our country and the passage of the hurricane. I had never experienced anything like that before, and my grandmother's house was ill prepared in the face of such a powerful storm. Hurricane Joan was a long-lasting phenomenon that caused death and destruction in more than a dozen countries in the Caribbean and Central America. It moved westward for nearly two weeks.

In October 1988, over the course of several weeks, Hurricane Joan wreaked havoc, causing floods and claiming over 200 lives as it passed through Central America.

On the night of October 22, Hurricane Joan, also known as Mirian, made landfall as a Category Four hurricane on the

Atlantic coast near Bluefields, causing massive devastation. My grandmother and I listened attentively to the information provided on the radio. She made coffee and began gathering the most important things, packing them into large plastic bags. After a long wait, she sent me to sleep. I don't recall closing my eyes due to the noise of the winds, trees, and the atmosphere. That early morning of the 23rd is etched in my mind. I distinctly remember silently crying out, "God, please help us, I'm scared." I didn't hear a response, but I could see it after the storm passed. Our little home had suffered minor damage, and my grandmother, our neighbors, and I were all safe. That night, I learned to communicate with God, and that day I discovered His existence because it was the first time I experienced His protection.

My Heavenly Father worked in a way that only He can. When the hurricane reached our area, the prayers of the evangelicals, who many considered crazy for their fervent vigil, were answered because Joan—a Category Four hurricane—transformed into a tropical depression upon entering the Nicaraguan Pacific. Our neighbors were safe, and together, we organized ourselves so that we could clean, cook, and help one another. The phone lines were out of service, and we couldn't communicate with our relatives, but gradually, things began to return to normal.

Some time after that experience, my parents decided it was time for me to live with them, and thus I was separated from my grandmother, with whom I had lived since the beginning of my life. That was one of my first emotional conflicts: I wanted to be with my parents and my sister, who was born while I was living in León, but I didn't want to leave my grandmother. The bus journey from León to Managua was far from easy; I cried a lot. While my mom reacted with frustration, my dad hugged me and reassured me that everything would be fine; his embrace brought me comfort. In my parents' house, I lacked absolutely nothing; however, the one person who had meant everything to me was not there.

This experience helped me understand what a child goes through when they are removed from one home and placed in another without explanations, without understanding what is happening. The anxiety this change can generate can last a lifetime, and the profound sadness that stems from this experience can eventually turn into depression.

My dad understood that it would be a long process of adaptation, but my mom wanted this process to be quick. She constantly asked me if I loved her and if I was happy with her; My silence in response to those questions didn't help at all.

The transition was also challenging for my sister, as she went from being the sole child to suddenly having to share everything. Thankfully, she has always been someone who naturally adapts quickly to new things. Within a few months of living together, we were inseparable.

As time went on, I was able to adjust to the change and to the routines of my family. My dad had his own law office, and my mom had already established a hair salon and a cafeteria which generated a good income.

Even though the country was going through difficult times, my parents had achieved a lot. My mom's businesses were located next to the Diplomatic Store, which was well-known and where only foreigners and government officials could shop. Many of the store's employees were customers at my mom's hair salon, and she obtained permission to make purchases at this store where payments were made in dollars and they sold all brands of toys and clothing from the United States. I loved seeing the Barbies and their enormous houses, and I enjoyed numerous sweets. In the store's parking lot, there were kids my age with buckets and towels, ready to wash cars. Very few times did I leave the store without sharing the candies I had bought. I became friends with some of them, and together with a lady named Antonia, known as Doña Toñita, who lived in the same neighborhood, we organized dinners, distributed candies, and read the Bible.

God showed me at an early age that my interest in social and community work was part of my life's purpose. I didn't know it at the time, but today I can see how He opened doors for me and gave me opportunities to participate in various social endeavors to serve and help others.

My mom generated more income than my dad, and that started to become a problem at home. She made her own travel arrangements, and my father made his plans separately. They lived together, they were together, but they weren't a married couple. I believe that the problems that had occurred even before I was born were never resolved, on the contrary, they worsened and ensnared my sister and me into the consequences.

My dad didn't seem very interested in exercising any kind of leadership at home. I am writing this not to judge my parents because I love both of them very much, and I know that they both gave what they had in them to give.

They both showed love as it had been shown to them. My father tried to be the father figure he had experienced: a silenced father, undermined, consumed by habits and behaviors that eventually caught up to him with significant repercussions. My mother tried to be the provider and hardworking woman that her own mother had been; she wasn't accustomed to showing or receiving love because she had a very difficult childhood. She showed her love through work and providing for her family. Her work ethic and effort were great examples for her daughters.

I now realize that my family was a group of orphans in search of the heart of a Father, in search of love, identity, guidance, acceptance, forgiveness, and healing.

When I found the heart of the Father through Jesus, I realized that I couldn't go through life blaming everyone for the troubles, situations, or injustices that had happened to me because my Heavenly Father promises that everything works together for the good of those who love Him (Romans 8:28)

As time passed, I noticed that even in the toughest situations, He has always been there, ready to help me and show me how great His love for me has been. Surrendering to the Heavenly Father has not been an easy task; I had to let go of many things that grew within me as a result of what others had planted, things that I had chosen to nurture and maintain. The lies I had accepted had obstructed my way for a long time, but God never gave up on me.

God confirmed what my father had told me in the hospital. When he passed away, I sought comfort for not having spent more time with him, for never having received answers to my numerous questions. On many occasions, I sought refuge in biblical reading and prayer; In one of those moments of reflection, God gave me this beautiful verse:

"Yet I came by and saw you there, kicking about in your blood, and as you lay there in your blood, I said to you, 'Live!' I made you grow like a plant in the field. You grew up and developed and became the most beautiful of jewels." Ezekiel 16:6-7a (NTV)

This verse reminds me of the words my father spoke to me during his illness, and today I recognize that my Heavenly Father tells me the same; as I write my story, I realize that if I flourish, it's because He was present, and even when few cared about my birth, He said, "Live."

CHAPTER 2
THE WOUND OF REJECTION

In starting this chapter, I want to explore the distinction between rejection and abandonment. While both can be encountered in the context of orphanhood, it's important to understand that one can be a consequence of the other.

For example, rejection is to repel someone, to cast them out; like in school, the message behind "You are an orphan" was actually: "Go away, we don't want you with us; we don't want to play with orphans." Although the intention was mockery, in my mind, it was perceived as: "They don't like me because I'm not like them. They don't accept me because I don't have parents."

At a very young age, I began to experience firsthand these social prejudices without even understanding their definitions. This rejection led me to don a mask of withdrawal, isolating myself from others and being cautious about engaging in situations, places, or relationships that didn't feel safe. I instinctively sought to protect myself from the possibility of further hurt.

In the definition of abandonment, we can find that it is the act of not only leaving someone behind to pursue something else, but it is also expressed in an idea or thought that takes root in the mind and heart of a child or an adult, as we can experience abandonment at any stage of our lives. This thought may manifest as, "I cannot have you with me" or "I cannot be with you." Various neurological studies assert that we can encounter abandonment and rejection even while nestled in the womb of our mother.

Just when I thought I was overcoming the weight of rejection, when I was beginning to feel secure within a family and immensely happy alongside my sister, my parents' relationship started to deteriorate to the point of separation. My father became involved in an extramarital affair and, as a result, made the decision to leave our home. The young woman he departed with gave birth to a baby boy just a few months later. Although my sister and I were delighted with the arrival of a little brother, we couldn't ignore how our father's interaction with us had changed.

During this time, my mother also decided to make travel and business plans, delegating our care to individuals she had hired, believing they would do a good job of looking after us while she was out of the country. My mother chose not to leave my grandmother in charge, and we paid a high price for that prideful decision.

We had no say or vote in what happened in our home, and although my father was in the country, he was living his new life, abandoning the responsibility of two teenagers who were going through significant physical and emotional changes. We suffered greatly from mistreatment by these individuals who mistakenly believed that we had no one who cared about our well-being. When we communicated the reality of our situation to my mother, with the help of my grandmother and one of my uncles, my mother became convinced that she needed to return and entrust our care to our grandmother. It was heartbreaking for me to see how both of our parents wanted to live their own lives while we were in the midst of adolescence, without their presence, love, supervision, and care.

As is often the case when teenagers are seeking attention and support, I became rebellious, aggressive, and always ready to take care of myself. During that time, all hope of my parents being present faded away in my heart.

In group therapy sessions that I have facilitated, many individuals have shared that they have experienced rejection at one or multiple stages of their lives. Some expressed that they sought to protect themselves from rejection by wearing masks of behavior. I can relate to this; I wore the mask of withdrawal. The girl who bullied me left a mark on my childhood. It affected my socialization with other girls; not only did she mock me, but she also organized others to mock and insult me. I began to put on the mask of reclusion as soon as I noticed similar behaviors in my interactions with others. Having experienced aggression, it became ingrained in me that confrontation would be one of my defense mechanisms in such situations.

Rejection also led me to become withdrawn in certain areas of my life, while being active and vocal in others. I felt that I had no value in the eyes of my parents, so I tried to be perfect in order to earn that value I believed was lacking. A person who believes they can do nothing right in their parents' eyes strives for perfection in everything, even if it entails unnecessary expenditure of energy and working tirelessly to earn self-worth. During a period of my youth,

I found it easier to make male friends than female friends. Distrust and fear welled up within me, originating from a vulnerable moment when that little girl discovered that my parents didn't live with me, a fact I had inadvertently shared with her.

At one point, she managed to gain my trust, and I confided in her, only to have her later exploit that very information against me. It was then that I realized I had unwittingly granted her power over me by revealing such personal details.

Unconsciously, the possibility that all my friends could betray me in that way had formed in my mind. So, to avoid pain and mockery, I began to share the fantastical visions that played out in my mind. And miraculously, Some of those longings that I yearned for with my parents became a reality. Today, I can say that I don't even remember this girl's name, with whom I shared a classroom for two years, but I remember vividly the damage her actions and words caused me. Sadly, perhaps she herself experienced situations at home that led her to behave that way towards others. Children learn more from what they see than from what they are told. They may behave aggressively towards others as a way to confront emotional situations and express inner anger, frustration, and confusion.

In adolescence, I began to feel that I was worthless, I was dissatisfied with myself because I had no idea of who I truly was. Like many young people, I was searching for my identity. It wasn't easy for me to say, "I resemble my father in this or that," because I didn't know him. On the other hand, in my mothers case, I could readily identify with her temperament and her less than desirable traits.

Much later, during therapy sessions, I realized that I resemble her a lot in her work ethic and determination. I put in effort at school, achieving the highest grades in the classroom. I received international awards at the Embassy of Venezuela in Nicaragua, serving as the president of an environmental movement and a student leader at my high school, but none of this fulfilled me. I didn't have my parents, and my sister was my sole support in many of these accomplishments. I began seeking acceptance and love in the wrong places and with the wrong people.

I sought refuge in my imaginary garden and allowed my fears to torment me. In my mind, people were temporary because I had never had someone constant in my life. Many psychologists and therapists describe these experiences as wounds of rejection. My life was the opposite of what God designed for a family. I lacked meaningful relationships and feared establishing them out of the sole fear of rejection. I only socialized with people with whom I felt completely safe and even then, I maintained a cautious distance and refrained from forming close bonds, driven by an overwhelming fear of rejection or abandonment—a consequence of lacking a stable figure in my life.

My intention was not to be antisocial, but to protect myself from pain. These experiences led me to understand that rejection is an emotional wound that can endure in someone's heart for a long time, perhaps without knowing how or when it happened.

Many people come to realize the origin of their rejection when they seek counseling or therapy to talk to someone and self-evaluate, thus finding the root of the problem. Through this process, there are habits or behaviors that can be eradicated, modified, or surrendered to God, as one recognizes the impact these behaviors have on their life and relationships. In my case, it took years, enduring pain, and disappointment to understand why I had defense mechanisms against rejection. For many years, I thought I was an orphan because I was rejected, but in reality, it was the rejection that gave rise to my feelings of orphanhood. Feeling rejected can lead us to develop emotional orphanhood, which means that even if both our parents are alive, the feeling of orphanhood and loneliness can lead us to live as orphans, walking without the emotional support of parents, without identity or direction. Knowing this, I cannot blame my parents for continuing the cycle of orphanhood in our family. We must remember that love is not just occasionally speaking kindly to our children or providing for their monetary and immediate needs; love should be demonstrated through emotional and spiritual action, with words that give life and actions that make our children feel secure and loved.

My parents simply shaped the love they had received. From a young age, I vowed to be different with my children, to break the cycle of emotional orphans in my family; I vowed that they would not go through the same path of rejection that affects their identity, self-esteem, relationships with others, and above all, their relationship with God. I also vowed that they would know God as their Father, understanding that they are never alone and that He loves them far more than I could ever do.

MY MOTHER AND REJECTION

My mother had a childhood filled with abuse and mistreatment. Like me, she experienced the separation of her parents: her father suddenly left the house, taking her sister with him and leaving her behind with a mother who suffered from various emotional disorders as a result of another childhood filled with maternal rejection, sexual abuse, a forced marriage at the age of fifteen, and many other things that marked her life. My mother always avoids recalling the day her father left because she still feels the pain that he didn't fight for her or take her with him. Her father provided a comfortable life for her sister, paid for her university education, and was always there to support her. My mother always says, "I wanted to go with my dad." and you can hear the pain in her voice when she says it. You can see the cycle of three generations living the same experiences of rejection and abandonment from one or both parents.

The good news is that this cycle ended when Jesus entered our lives. My sister and I have decided to raise our children in a completely different way, with parenting styles that I will explain in the next chapter. We have chosen to follow God's life manual for the family to the best of our abilities. There is no perfect parenting, but God teaches us that love covers a multitude of faults, and in His immense grace, He helps us to love others above ourselves. I decided to fill my heart with the love of God, which helped me to forgive my mother and heal wounds that have impacted my life. I can't say that occasional thoughts or concerns don't try to enter my mind, or that I don't have any emotional triggers.

When there is any difference of opinions between my mother and me, God gives me discernment to determine the right timing to talk about these things and when it's not. He teaches me to renew my mind and guard myself from memories or thoughts that may hinder the growth of my relationship with my mother. He has also helped me establish healthy boundaries in many areas.

I believe that one of the things that affects orphans the most is not knowing their story.

When parents speak to their children honestly about their past it facilitates forgiveness, compassion for what they have been through, and it allows the child to love them without judgment or complaints; But when parents ignore these conversations and put up shields filled with justifications, lies, pride, and arrogance, it leads to anger, bitterness, and creates a void separating them from their children, allowing resentment, and a lack of forgiveness to fester within them. Children are not judges of their parents, but we have the right to know our history. When I became a mother, I started asking why they chose to leave me because I couldn't imagine giving away my newborn baby.

My mother didn't answer any questions; instead, she justified herself by saying that my grandmother arrived at the hospital and convinced her that I would be better off with her and that she would take better care of me. Today, I can see that it was her desire to establish a relationship with her own mother and the desire to feel accepted and loved by her that made her easily manipulable to her wishes. The emotional manipulation from generation to generation between mothers and daughters has been another outcome of rejection, one that would later affect our own relationship. There are many things that don't make sense, but when I stopped searching for the truth about my parents and held on to God, focusing on his benevolent plans for my life that were created even before my existence in my mother's womb, I became less interested in the past and more focused on what God had established for me.

Discovering God as a present Father, the ultimate Provider, infused my wounded heart, scarred by rejection and the void of a father, with inner healing. God has given me a peace that surpasses all understanding. He has helped me pray and present every concern regarding my childhood, adolescence, and current life. He has been with me every step of the way and continues to reveal the life He designed for me, my identity in Him, and my purpose in this world. God has made everything new and filled my heart with His love.

After praying for the ability to have difficult conversations with my mother, she responded to some concerns that helped us grow emotionally and heal together. God has taught me to extend the same mercy that I desire to receive from Him to others and has shown me how challenging it can be to transition from orphans to children. With God, nothing is impossible, but the decision to heal and be free from the chains of rejection is in our hands. In reality, my mother and father were seeking the same thing as I was: the love of the Father.

MY FATHER AND REJECTION

My father grew up with both parents, but it was his mother who made all the decisions at home. His father was silenced by the matriarch of the household. For my father, it was not unusual for a woman to take charge of everything at home. He had an older brother, and his mother openly expressed favoritism towards her younger son, my dad.

She took care of every detail of my father's life, even when he was an adult. When he started a relationship with my mother, she felt entitled to dictate what they should do. Any woman who entered the family had to submit to her way of doing things. None would be worthy enough if they didn't get along with her. My mother came into my father's life, and the first thing she experienced was the rejection from her mother-in-law, and once again, the male figure who was supposed to defend her from the attacks abandoned her during her pregnancy.

My grandfather was never present in the lives of his children, despite living with them. I believe he had come to the conclusion that if his opinion didn't matter, there was no need to express it. This behavior was repeated by my father in his relationship with my mother. Like my father, my grandfather sought refuge in harmful defense mechanisms and justified his absence with work. My father was following the model he had been given, and, like my mother, he aimed to give his best without exposing his mistakes or telling the truth. He preferred to remain silent until his last days rather than saying something that could hurt me or damage the image of my mother.

God granted me the opportunity to take care of him during his illness. We had long conversations and realized that we had a lot in common. I spoke to him about God at every opportunity, letting him know that I had forgiven him and was grateful to God for being able to be by his side. My father thanked me for not rejecting him and for going to Nicaragua to take care of him. He apologized for all the decisions he had made in the past and for his absence. My mother was in Miami, and my father wanted to see her to ask for forgiveness. I believe that both of them needed to forgive each other, although my mother didn't see it that way. Pride and resentment often keep us blindfolded and chained in our hearts. When I went to Miami with my mother, I explained my father's delicate condition to her. I also took the opportunity to remind her that both of them had made many mistakes. The intention was not to bring someone to be humiliated but to be forgiven. God was greatly glorified by bringing my parents together. We prayed, had dinner together, and spent quality time as a family.

We took photos, they spent time alone, and both could see that despite everything, God never abandoned them or me. They realized that in the end, the only thing that truly matters is being right with God and loving others, focusing on the goodness in people rather than the pain that has been passed down from generation to generation. God is faithful to His Word, and through Jesus, He breaks every generational chain of rejection in the lives of His children.

The death of my earthly father gave birth to a new relationship with my Heavenly Father, who comforted me, loved me, and provided everything I needed to overcome the pain of loss and the difficult processes in my marital life. The fatherhood of God is sufficient to give us healing and wholeness in life and in the body; He provides the physical and spiritual healing that so many of us seek.

'Though my father and mother forsake me, the Lord will receive me.' Psalm 27:10 NIV"

CHAPTER 3
PARENTING STYLES

In the previous chapter, we observed some of the behaviors, traumas, and family dynamics that affected my childhood and adolescence regarding rejection. In this chapter, I will present how our childhood experiences, traumas, fears, and situations, accompanied by the type of upbringing our parents or grandparents provided, have a significant impact on our development as individuals. Just like me, my parents had a set of different parenting styles that also influenced their behavior.

We witnessed the importance of speaking to our children with truth, and that leads me to think about the times when we share our own childhood anecdotes; And even though we see discrepancies in the story, we don't feel the courage or confidence to ask those questions.

My purpose is not to encourage questioning everything we are told, but to promote honest conversations filled with love and respect between parents and children. Do you know why it is different when someone tells a story from the time they were days or months old? It's the trust we have in the person who told us how we were when we were born, or in my case, when my grandmother decided to raise me. We then walk through life believing in these stories; they become part of our identity until someone else comes along with their own version.

Depending on the version we are told, we have three options:
1. Believe the first version
2. Believe the second version
3. Believe God's truth.

In this final point, I want to share that God revealed the truth to me. As His Word teaches, I came to know the truth, and it set me free (John 8:32). This truth is not merely a concept, but a person who embodies it: Jesus.

There are many parts of my early life story that did not unfold the way I was told, but the negative emotions from not knowing the truth were healed by God's truth. God's truth created a new identity in me, a new purpose: it transformed me from being an orphan to being a daughter. It is difficult to explain the feeling of freedom I experienced when I understood that I am the daughter of a loving Father who has been with me through every stage of my life.

God has been the father I longed for, affirming His immense love for me despite my mistakes. He is the Father who has known me even before the very beginning of this world and he knows everything there is to know about me. With Him, there is no need to wear masks or try to please Him in all the ways I can, for nothing satisfies Him. He only desires my heart and genuine repentance for anything I have done contrary to His truth. Through His Word, He guides us in life and provides the necessary counsel to hold onto His hand and face any situation.

In the realm of parenting styles, we can discern parallels to the way in which God shapes our lives, nurtures our faith, and guides us toward fulfilling His purpose. He employs discipline and correction as necessary, yet He remains unwavering in His love for us and never forsakes us. Jesus has never rejected me for being a woman, He has had no expectations of me, and when I fail to meet them, He does not distance Himself as an earthly father might do. There is nothing in the heavens nor on earth that can separate me from him. His love is so great that he gives me the gift of choice, of being able to decide between having a close relationship with Him or living a life without Him, and even though I have often rejected Him, like the prodigal son, when I returned home, He threw a celebration to welcome me back. God has used many teachers, brothers and sisters in faith, and special people to reveal the identity He designed for me: an identity marked by daughterhood, not orphanhood.

One day, during my prayer, I received a beautiful revelation that emphasized the significance of recognizing God's fatherhood in order to truly comprehend the depth of His love for us and His desire for us to fulfill His plans. The thought resonated within me, " When you don't know who you are, you will become what others tell you to be." This truth struck me profoundly, as for numerous years, I sought refuge in the fictional narratives of others and my own imaginary world, seeking solace from the pain, ridicule, and rejection I experienced. I became what others wanted me to be, influenced by the trends of this world and not the identity for which I was designed by the architect of the universe.

As parents, it is crucial for us to prioritize the holistic development of our children, encompassing their social, emotional, and spiritual growth. By creating a nurturing environment that fosters their identity and cultivates these areas of their lives, we enable them to flourish and thrive.

Can we attain perfection as parents? Absolutely not. However, with God's guidance, supported by His word and prayer, we can strive to honor Him by giving our utmost in raising our precious children.

We, as parents, can strive to do everything within our reach and trust that God will do what is not possible for us, for what is impossible for humans is possible for God (Luke 18:27). Let's examine how society defines orphanhood and family relationships.

The Oxford dictionary defines the word as follows:

1. Noun, a person who does not have a father, mother, or both because they have passed away. "to be orphaned"

2. Adjective That lacks a thing, quality, or necessary characteristic, especially some form of protection or assistance that one should enjoy.

Based on my personal experience, I can affirm that this is the essence of the word "orphan." And if, like me, you have encountered the second definition, feeling devoid of protection or support despite having living parents, we may relate to and even perceive it as the reality of our lives.

However, if we opt to embrace God's truth, we will arrive at a profound realization: our thinking can be transformed and revitalized through His Word.

"The father of the fatherless and the protector of widows is God in his holy habitation. God settles the solitary in a home; he leads the prisoners to prosperity." Psalms 68:5-6

Let's consider some definitions that society has determined for family relationships.

1. Father: A father is the male progenitor with paternal ties to his children. The father can have a biological, emotional, legal, and social relationship with the child that entails certain rights, obligations, and responsibilities.

2. Children: Individuals connected in relation to their biological or adoptive parents. Also, children of a nation.

3. Mother: A mother is the female parent of a child. A woman with a biological or emotional relationship. This woman can be considered a mother by giving birth, raising a child who may or may not be her biological offspring, or by providing her egg for fertilization in the case of surrogacy.

4. Siblings: Individuals with bonds, considered in relation to each other, who are children of the same parents or at least share the same father or mother.

I consider it very important that each of these terms includes the word "relationship" to establish the connection between parents and children and among family members. That is what many of us are seeking in life.

I always felt that something was missing, and that something was a relationship with God. Establishing a Father-daughter relationship with Him has led me to healing and forgiveness, and that's how I was able to have a relationship with my father and mother. To break free from emotional chains and the negative cycles that took place in my family, it was necessary for me to study parenting styles and compare them with what the Bible says about fatherhood and motherhood. Understanding the role of each family member is crucial in establishing healthy relationships.

PARENTING STYLES

1. Authoritarian Parents

They are inflexible, demanding, and strict when it comes to controlling behavior. They have many rules. They expect obedience and authority. They favor severe or excessive punishment as a way to control their children's behavior. Their children tend to be irritable, apprehensive, fearful, moody, unhappy, irritable, ill-tempered, prone to stress, and lacking in motivation for self-improvement.

"And you, fathers, do not provoke your children to anger, but bring them up in the discipline and instruction of the Lord." Ephesians 6:4 (NBLA)

Proverbs 22:15 tells us that the heart of young people is filled with foolishness. It acknowledges the role of physical discipline in redirecting their inclination towards potentially harmful behaviors. There is much written about the adverse effects of physical abuse on children's mental health, but the Bible does not call us to use abusive or harmful correction but to exercise authority, which may sometimes involve physical punishment. Firmly and authoritatively removing our children from a dangerous situation, raising our voice with firmness, and taking away physical privileges such as being part of a desired social gathering is physical correction without harming them. I want to clarify that I do not disapprove of occasional physical correction, provided that it does not cross the line into abuse and is appropriate for the age of the children involved.

I was a very mischievous child, and although my grandmother did her best and applied what she knew, I would touch everything. And once I touched something that was unacceptable to my grandmother: her famous wardrobe. I took out an object that caught my attention and tried to open it, but in the process, I broke it. My grandmother grabbed my hands and said:

"If you touch anything again, I'll burn your hands." As she placed my hands very close to the stove.

Although she didn't burn me, the terror of being so close caused me anxiety; it took years for me to share that memory. When that image came to my mind in adulthood, it created feelings of helplessness and anger. I blamed my parents for not protecting me and allowing it to happen, even though it was culturally acceptable in many places. My grandmother could go from being the most tender and kind person to an irritated, angry, and hostile individual when she administered punishments.

One day, while conducting an assessment with a very young girl, I noticed behaviors similar to what I experienced when I was punished. God allowed me to see that day how we can use the terrible experiences in our lives to help others. I began asking the girl some questions, and my supervisor made a decision in that case based on clinical interventions and the responses to the inquiries. Indeed, the girl was experiencing physical abuse, neglect, and emotional mistreatment.

2. Parents with authority

These parents are affectionate and supportive towards their child, but at the same time, they establish firm boundaries. They try to control their children's behavior through rules, dialogue, and reasoning with them. The discipline they exercise is based on principles that benefit the children, the parents, and strengthen sibling relationships. They listen to their children's opinions even when they disagree.

As a result, children tend to be friendly, energetic, independent, curious, self-controlled, cooperative, and driven to establish goals and plans that lead to success.

3. Permissive parents

These parents are affectionate but relaxed and do not establish firm boundaries. They do not closely monitor their children's activities or demand appropriate behavior in different situations. As a result, children tend to be impulsive, rebellious, aimless, dominant, aggressive, with low self-esteem, lack of self-control, and little motivation to achieve success.

Boundaries are necessary in our lives. Although we may sometimes wish to be friends or colleagues with our children, the reality is that we cannot. It is not healthy for us to act like our children or for them to act like parents. Effective parenting requires us to set limits and rules at home, starting from a young age. The established rules should have a balance, as having no rules is dangerous, but overly strict rules can also be harmful.

The rules should apply equally to all children, without molding them based on individual personalities. If one child breaks a rule, it is essential that both receive the same correction.

If we show flexibility towards one child but adopt strictness with the other, it will inevitably impact our relationship with them and their overall well-being. This dynamic can lead teenagers to question our parental authority and harbor resentment towards their siblings. Over time, this resentment may transform into feelings of bitterness, jealousy, and envy.

It is vital for us to be mindful of how our children respond to the rules we establish and to listen to them attentively, just as we would with our friends. Furthermore, we should exercise the compassion that God grants us, always bearing in mind that we will be held accountable for the responsibility of their education one day.

Discipline is never pleasant at the time when receiving it. On the contrary, it is painful! But afterwards, it yields the peaceful harvest of a righteous life for those who have been trained by it (Hebrews 12:11).

4. Passive parents

They exhibit indifference, inaccessibility, and a predisposition towards rejection. As a result, their children often struggle with low self-esteem, lack of self-confidence, a dearth of ambition, and sometimes seek inappropriate role models in an attempt to fill the void left by their neglectful parents. Passive parents may also be absent from their children's lives, and in their quest for attention, many children display behaviors such as aggression, diminished self-worth, and heightened fearfulness. Furthermore, these children may become more susceptible to bullying or may themselves engage in bullying as a means to alleviate the emotional frustrations they experience.

In my work with young people, I have encountered those who have expressed their thoughts in this way:

"If my parents show no concern for me, why should I expect you to care?"

This statement holds significant emotional significance as it is often a driving force behind people turning away from God. It is essential to grasp the concept of God as a loving Father in order to comprehend that everything we do carries immense importance to Him. He does not pass judgment or reject us; instead, He guides us and rejoices in our daily victories, regardless of their magnitude. He is always present! Not as a permissive Father, but an everloving father who sets rules, statutes, and boundaries for our own good. Now, let's delve into some examples of behaviors that we can observe in adults, which trace their origins back to childhood experiences.

- **From the age of eight, Teresita assumed the responsibility of caring for her younger siblings, who were five and six years old at the time.** Following her parents' separation, with her mother leaving home and her father working long hours to support the family, Teresita did her utmost to fulfill the role of a mother figure at home. She would prepare her siblings for the day, ensuring they were ready for school, making breakfast for them, helping them bathe, and accompanying them to school. Upon their return, she refrained from joining other children in playtime; instead, she would wash their uniforms, prepare dinner for the family, and assist her siblings with their homework.

Today, as an adult with her own family, Teresita has accomplished much and excelled in various areas. However, she grapples with a reluctance to seek assistance and carries the constant burden of caring for her siblings, which often leads to anxiety and high levels of stress. Additionally, she has faced challenges in her relationships with her siblings, particularly in situations involving financial needs where she struggles to provide for both her siblings and her own family.

These examples serve as illustrations of how our early experiences and the responsibilities we shoulder can significantly influence our behaviors and attitudes in adulthood. They demonstrate the enduring impact of childhood roles and shed light on the difficulties individuals may encounter as they navigate the delicate balance between tending to their own needs and fulfilling the caring and supportive roles they have assumed for others.

- **Miriam grew up in a family with a very strict and emotionally repressive father, leaving little room for the expression of opinions and ideas.** In such an environment, Miriam's mother found herself unable to voice her own perspectives in matters requiring decision-making, as her father exerted control over every aspect of their lives. Miriam grew up subjected to derogatory remarks about women and father dismissed her whenever she expressed something she had learned at school. Her father held the belief that investing in Miriam's education was unnecessary, solely because she was a girl and would eventually marry, start a family, and become dependent on her husband. He emphasized the importance of her marrying a wealthy man.

Throughout her adolescence, Miriam faced significant challenges in finding ways to express her true feelings. As an adult, she has made progress in overcoming social isolation, yet she continues to work on identifying and articulating her emotions with clarity and precision.

- **Gabriel, as an only child, grew up in a nurturing environment with both of his parents, granting him abundant opportunities throughout his childhood.**

However, his parents' excessive protection hindered his independence, as they took charge of various aspects of his life. They assisted him with his academic responsibilities and demanded that he achieve high grades without exceptions. Consequently, Gabriel developed a tendency to push himself excessively, leading to chronic stress within his professional life.

As an adult, Gabriel grapples with anxiety, harboring various fears and seeking security primarily through relationships. He has developed codependency on many occasions, which has strained his relationships with other adults in his social circle.

- **Antonio grew up with both parents; however, many things that happened in his family were never clearly explained to him.** In order to make him feel better, his parents and other family members would lie to him and make promises that were never fulfilled. Today, Antonio experiences a high level of difficulty in trusting others. When he engages in social circles, he questions others, and even though he listens quietly, his body language shows that he is analyzing what others are saying, creating a sense of mistrust in return. He admits that he is ready to respond and confront people, and this has led him to experience social isolation on many occasions.

Johana grew up in a home where her mother made all the decisions. Whenever her father wanted to speak, express an opinion, or make a different decision, he was silenced. It was clear to Johana and her siblings that their father was only present to provide for the family and nothing more. He was publicly humiliated to ensure that everyone knew the woman was in charge at home.

Despite this dynamic, Johana's father showed his love through quality time and enjoyed taking his children out of their daily routine. He would take them to different towns, teaching them history and exposing them to new experiences whenever he had the opportunity. He motivated Johana to be a good student and encouraged her to have dreams and goals.

On the other hand, Johana's mother was not emotionally expressive. She focused on her work and prioritized her professional pursuits over family matters. All the resources she produced went towards her businesses and projects. Meanwhile, Johana's father took care of the household expenses and the upbringing of the children. Johana's mother saved money out of fear of her husband leaving her, abandoning her, or being unfaithful. During Johana's adolescence, her mother influenced her in a different way, instilling a fear and mistrust of men, saying, "You have to prepare yourself because you can't trust men, they're all the same."

Johana struggled for many years with secondary traumas that her mother passed on to her. Her mother came from a long line of single women raising children on their own, and even though this wasn't her situation, she had a deep-seated fear that the same could happen to her; and this affected the family dynamics of her children and her relationship with their father. As a result, Johana experienced many breakups, divorces, and negative experiences in her relationships with men. She didn't know how to trust them and saw them as untrustworthy. The fear of rejection overshadowed the love that led her to establish meaningful connections.

However, Johana made a decision to renew her mind and focus on her spiritual growth and relationship with God. Through studying Scriptures and understanding her true identity, Johana understood that submitting to a husband is not the erroneous concept that had been presented to her.

In the early stages of development, a child is not yet capable of comprehending that they have been entrusted to another adult for care, or that they may have experienced rejection or abandonment. A young child possesses a great resilience and forms attachments to the person meeting their basic needs. Let's note that shelter, food, education, and clothing cover physical needs, but without the necessary emotional and spiritual nourishment, children grow up lacking the tools to navigate their questions, comparisons, depression, anxiety, and other emotional ailments that begin to arise as they grow and develop. Often, this is the transitional stage between childhood and adolescence, where if we don't know who God is and how His fatherhood operates in our lives, we may find ourselves placing blame on Him for everything that has happened to us.

For a long time, I struggled with what people around me said about my mother. My moms neighbors and some relatives took every opportunity to tell me that she had left me to go partying or, as they say in Nicaragua, "to go to bacanal." When I asked what a bacanal was, people laughed; I didn't know if they were laughing at me for not understanding them or because I had been abandoned.

Being mocked as a child is yet another way that I experienced rejection. It caused immense confusion and profound sadness within me, leading to the accumulation of resentment, anger, self-esteem issues, feelings of rejection, anxiety, depression, and pride. Whenever I read the Gospel of Luke 8:2, which recounts the liberation of Mary Magdalene from seven demons, I can relate to the spiritual and emotional bondages that Jesus has also freed me from.

During my childhood, I used to cry frequently, and I vividly recall a family member telling me, "Shut up, Magdalene."

One night, as I was reading my Bible, this passage sought to enter my mind. The memory of the shouting and mockery was accompanied by an accusing thought: "You are just as sinful as she is." However, in that moment, another thought quickly followed: "Just as she was set free, so have you been. The old things have passed away; behold, all things have become new." God's wonders are boundless; the more we seek Him, the clearer His voice becomes to us.

I believe it is of utmost importance to integrate support groups and moments of solitude with God into therapy. It is through these avenues that we can receive the healing that only He can provide. God shows us the truth, embraces us, and reveals our true identities and purpose.

Another strategy of this world that deeply affects us is comparison. It is crucial for adults to be mindful of what they say in front of children, even when they think the children are not paying attention or won't understand. I heard hurtful comments like, "They abandoned Claudia and then she gave birth to another daughter."

These words caused division among siblings and made me feel betrayed by my parents.

Despite the initial discomfort, I grew accustomed to having my little sister around, and we developed a bond of playing and running together. God has been gracious in helping us maintain a relationship amidst the challenges we have faced together. In the past, I used to assume that everything was fine with her because she was at home. I thought, "She's with mom and dad, she has everything she needs, and she's okay." It was in adulthood that we were finally able to discuss the separate experiences we went through. I was struck when she shared that she witnessed numerous fights, arguments, and marital problems between our parents, which also left a lasting impact on her. Although my sister spent some time with me in León, she didn't live there, and the pain I felt when we were separated ran deep.

A child who is left behind will feel betrayed, confused, rejected, and without any understanding of why it has happened. In other words, the confusion leads them to doubt whether they are truly loved or if they simply exist in this world with no one by their side.

Often in the Bible, God reveals Himself as "the God who sees me." Jesus said to Nathanael, "I saw you under the fig tree." God frequently used my teachers as instruments to convey messages to me: "I see your effort," "You are intelligent," "Keep striving," "Don't be afraid." The hugs I received from my teachers on Mother's Day, the poetry recitals, and the academic recognitions were all precious gifts from God. Looking back, I can now recognize that my Heavenly Father was present in those significant moments through the people He strategically placed in my life.

My sister's testimony has opened my eyes to the fact that we never truly know what someone is going through. It's easy to imagine that others have better lives than us, but the reality is that we have all experienced situations that have left a lasting impact. As she shared her story, I didn't rejoice at all; on the contrary, I could sense the sadness in her words as she recounted events that could have unfolded differently. Despite the challenges she faced, she has surrendered them to God and has become a source of healing for many, including myself, through her faith in Christ.

The Word of God tells us, "Do not conform to the pattern of this world, but be transformed by the renewing of your mind." These are among the multiple truths that God offers us to understand that spiritual and physical transformation begins in the mind. It is through this understanding that we recognize ourselves as beloved children, created with purpose and goals. The realization that God, our Father, is interested in every detail of our lives is vital for healing and assisting others in their healing journeys.

"Do not imitate the behavior and customs of this world, but let God transform you into a new person by changing the way you think. Then you will learn to know God's will for you, which is good, pleasing, and perfect."
Romans 12:2 (NLT)

CHAPTER 4

A JOURNEY INTO THE UNKNOWN

Accelerating responsibilities in children disrupts their natural development and hinders the gradual emotional growth essential for their overall well-being. When a child or adolescent is burdened with adult responsibilities, it compromises their ability to form secure attachments in future relationships. Supportive and nurturing parents play a crucial role in making children feel valued and understood, enabling them to navigate the challenges of adolescence, including the insecurities arising from physical changes. Conversely, children with unaffectionate or unstable parents, who must fend for themselves, develop insecure and unstable attachments.

Consequently, young individuals become susceptible to controlling, manipulative, or unscrupulous individuals who exploit this lack of love to create close relationships with those who are willing to do anything to find affection, acceptance, and love, even when it is evident that these relationships can be highly toxic and dangerous.

Children often face significant problems that are typically encountered in adulthood, which accelerates their maturity but deprives them of gradual emotional development that is essential for their wellbeing. Maturity is a gradual process, and imposing it prematurely leads to frustration and rebellion. Bypassing the stages of maturity can create behaviors and traumas that profoundly impact their mental well-being in adulthood. The child becomes fixated on fulfilling assigned responsibilities in hopes of earning affection or words of love from their parents.

Instead, they receive criticism and disdain, resulting in emotional wounds, low self-esteem, and a profound mistrust of others and themselves. Studies conducted by the American Psychological Association in the United States reveal that adults who did not receive love from their mothers during childhood develop a distorted belief that the world is inherently unsafe, and people harbor malicious intentions. Consequently, they struggle immensely with trust in friendships and close relationships.

"The child with ambivalent attachment requires constant validation that trust is guaranteed. These individuals experience love as an obsession, a desire for reciprocity and union, emotional ups and downs, and jealousy." - Cindy Hazan, psychologist.

Children with anxious or ambivalent attachment experience a constant sense of insecurity due to the inconsistent behaviors of their parents. As a facilitator of therapy groups focusing on anxiety, panic attacks, fears, and insecurities, I have observed how the physical or emotional absence of parents during childhood, toxic and abusive family relationships, orphanhood, and emotional abuse profoundly impact the lives of individuals who underwent accelerated growth without experiencing a adolescence guided by genuinely caring individuals concerned about their well-being.

After a turbulent childhood filled with the emotional pain of rejection and the physical absence of my parents, .I had to go through what many immigrants have experienced: leaving behind what they know in the hope of a positive change in their lives and the lives of their families in a new country; Despite their separation, my parents agreed that it was not in our best interest to be unsupervised under the care of our grandmother, who was seriously ill at the time. Neither of my parents wanted to acknowledge that neglectful caregiving had led us to seek love and acceptance in misguided places and, in my case, with the wrong people. Despite it all, God consistently protected me from making detrimental choices and saved me from dangers that could have profoundly altered my life in many ways. Today, I can confidently assert that every experience I went through was a valuable learning process, transformed into life lessons that now empower me to support young individuals and families. I firmly believe that God turned my mistakes into teachings, converting defeats into victories for the purpose of assisting others.

During that time, I was starting to search for love; I was attracted to slightly older youth, and like in many cases, I was falling into an abusive and very dangerous relationship. Seeking love, acceptance, and security, I unwittingly allowed manipulative and controlling behaviors to permeate my life. Eventually, I made the decision to end the two-year relationship, but the aftermath proved to be a harrowing ordeal. The young man, consumed by suicidal thoughts, arrived at my house one night and forcibly abducted me at gunpoint. He took me to a nearby park, where he aimed the gun at his own head before my eyes. At that moment, all I could think was, "God, please intervene." Despite my lack of knowledge and experience, God provided me with the words that snapped the young man out of his destructive mindset, and my family arrived in the nick of time. My father spoke with the young man's mother, and they agreed not to press charges on the condition that he would stay away from me. After that traumatizing experience, my parents made the decision to take me out of the country and relocate to Miami, where I would live with my mother.

We had visited Miami before, but this time everything was very different. I didn't know anyone, I didn't speak English, and the school system was completely different from what I was familiar with. Amidst all the newness, I felt a great relief to be living with my mother and the opportunity for a fresh start. We arrived at an apartment in Little Havana, on Southwest 7th Street; My sister and I could easily walk to the bodega on the famous Calle Ocho and explore the renowned Cuban bakeries together.

Despite being in the southwest, I was assigned to a school that had a negative reputation due to its location in the Allapattah area. My mother made countless efforts to prevent me from attending that school, but it was the designated one for our district. As a teenager, I became even more intrigued by this school because I was explicitly told not to go there. Curiosity overwhelmed me, and I was determined to find out why it was so widely discouraged. I deduced that its reputation stemmed from its location, the demographic makeup of its student body, and the lack of awareness about the school's performance within the community. Miami Jackson Senior High School captured my interest, so I sought advice from one of the clients at the hair salon, who encouraged us to visit the school.

Her daughter had already graduated from there, and this lady spoke highly of her experience. She advised me, saying, "Do your part, stay away from negative influences, and put in a great effort. That school has excellent teachers, and if you are a good student, you have nothing to fear." My mom went to enroll me, and to her surprise, the staff members who assisted her, although they didn't speak Spanish like the ones at the school she initially wanted, helped her complete all the necessary paperwork and connected us with a counselor who was fluent in Spanish. The counselor was firm and told us:

"It is very challenging to graduate without a strong command of English, given the difficulty of the state exam. But if you dedicate yourself and work hard, I believe you can achieve it. If you don't pass that exam, you may have to repeat twelfth grade, but we will support you and allow you to stay in your senior year."

It was a year filled with dedication and faith as I sought God's help to excel in school. I firmly believe that God has placed something extraordinary within me—a direct line to Him—especially when people declare, "It's difficult," "It's impossible," or "There's no cure," among many other things. I am deeply grateful to God because even when I didn't know Him, I relied on the gift of faith He had bestowed upon me. One particular verse from His Word that has continually inspired me to activate that faith:

"Jesus looked at them and said, 'Humanly speaking, it is impossible. But with God, everything is possible.'"
(Matthew 19:26, NLT)

My mom worked tirelessly and paid for a private bus since the one assigned by the school had a distant stop from the building. She wanted to take care of us, and while it may seem insignificant to some or seen as her duty, it meant a lot to me because it was the first time I was living with my mom full-time. We may not have had the same comforts we were accustomed to in Nicaragua, but in this new place, we had each other. I slept in the living room of the small apartment that my mom had acquired and lovingly prepared for our arrival. I was the first one picked up by the bus in the morning and the last one dropped off in the evening. My mom would accompany me every day, coming downstairs at 5:30 in the morning. It was on this bus that I met my first husband. He was also a senior in high school, and despite having arrived in Miami before me, he was struggling academically. He rarely attended school and had to put in a lot of effort, just like me, to graduate the following summer.

Although we both shared the goal of graduating, our reasons were quite different, yet we found ourselves in the same battle. He invited me to prom, and from there, we officially started dating, getting to know each other and making plans together. With time, we achieved our goal. After finishing school, he enlisted in the United States Marines or Marine Corps, while I began studying political science at Miami Dade Community College.

DANGEROUS LOVES

My experience in the United States taught me that even in the face of numerous obstacles, I can maintain my focus on a hopeful future. Like many young immigrants, I lacked a social security number and had no opportunities to utilize the hard-earned scholarships I had received. While there are now organizations that assist Hispanic students in such situations, that wasn't the case 23 years ago in South Florida. Assistance was primarily organized by country-specific groups, whereas nowadays, there are funds available for Latinos of all nationalities. As an aspiring student in the Armed Forces, I also sought to support my hardworking mother who was shouldering the burden of my education.

Both my sister and I assisted her at her hair salon and at home, but the mounting financial frustration began to strain our relationship. Neither my sister nor I had any interest in pursuing careers as stylists, and our resistance to our mother's plans only heightened the stress and differences between us. This further fueled my desire to leave home, mirroring the path my parents had taken in search of a different life.

In the midst of this situation, my boyfriend recognized my predicament and offered to help me break free from home. His plan was for us to marry once he completed his military training and start a new life together. These kinds of ideas often emerge among young people who seek solutions based on their own understanding of life. Depending on their age, some receive guidance and advice, while others do not. Many young individuals possess the ability to communicate with their parents and express their thoughts and feelings, but not all have that privilege.

This makes me think of how I used to solve my problems when I felt like an orphan in my childhood. Now, as an adolescent, I found myself without my parents' emotional support and guidance. I felt as though I was wandering aimlessly, relying solely on my own compass. I sought help, but nobody took the time to truly understand what was going on in my mind and heart. I became fixated on my immediate needs without considering the long-term consequences. I lived in a perpetual search for love, often complaining and becoming angry about the issues at home, consistently wearing the mask of rebellion and anger. Predictably, this relationship ended in divorce, as marriages founded on reasons other than genuine love often do.

This specific experience has motivated me, with the help of God and my husband Mario, to establish the Matthew 20 ministry, where I support young people, adults, and families as a mentor and counselor. In my practice, I use a combination of psychological, social, and spiritual interventions so that, together with the young people I serve, we can focus on uncovering, cultivating, and fortifying their inherent identities with which they have been created, rather than the distorted versions that life may have imposed upon them through their personal journeys, mistakes, traumas, and familial circumstances.

THE RELATIONSHIP WITH MY MOTHER

I firmly believe that honoring our parents is a divine commandment; I also know that God calls us not to provoke our children to anger. However, striking this balance is not always an easy task. It is crucial for fostering a healthy relationship between parents and children, yet it is not always practiced within our own homes. My mother has always been incredibly devoted to her work. However, as time went on, her dedication transformed into an obsession, and spending quality time with the family became less of a priority for her. Despite living in one of the world's most renowned cities, we rarely ventured out for leisure. Our days fell into a monotonous routine: school, the hair salon, and back home to repeat it all over again.

It was through school that I began to discover new places, and my involvement in the Army's ROTC program allowed me the opportunity to venture out and explore different parts of the city and the state of Florida. I started envisioning myself as a member of the United States military. Despite not having residency documents, my determination to serve propelled me to work diligently and pursue a path towards joining the military. I embarked on a quest for information on how to enlist, and the Marine Corps recruiter recognized my desire to serve and provided guidance on the document processing. At that time, we had already submitted applications to the immigration department. I had to endure a lengthy wait, but eventually, I was able to enlist in the United States Army and serve actively in the military.

You could say that my journey to the United States mirrors the experiences of what is now known as "Dreamers." In reality, I didn't decide to come here. In Nicaragua, I had become part of the student and community leadership. It was very difficult to leave my friends, my school, everything I knew, and start anew in a place with many limitations and fears. I firmly believe that God is in control of our lives, and I can clearly see how He has orchestrated everything for the well-being of me and my family. It was through our immigrant journey that we truly came to know God, and despite our imperfections and differences, we find solace in entrusting our problems into His hands. It has been through obstacles and physical, economic, and emotional hardships that we have come to know God, not only for what He gives us but for the loving Father that He is.

My mother was the one who provided most of what we consumed at home and took care of everything related to our well-being. She was also the one who had to face the immigration expenses to give us the opportunity to acquire a legal status and move forward. My frustrations, my mother's frustrations, and the unresolved emotional conflicts led to a turbulent relationship between us. We argued a lot, I felt a lot of anger towards her, and I didn't understand why. I started wearing the mask of rebellion, instead of expressing what I truly felt the desire to feel the love and involvement of my parents in my life, beyond mere material provisions, genuine love, not driven by obligation or concern for others' opinions of them as parents.

During counseling sessions, I have often encountered individuals who express deep sadness regarding their relationships with their parents. What pains them the most is when they perceive their parents adopting an attitude of entitlement: "They must love me because I have given them everything" or "they are obligated to consider my opinion because of what I sacrificed for them," without taking into account their children's feelings. In my case, my parents unconsciously ignored my pain, which ignited feelings of anger within me.

I perceived that my mother was focused on her dreams and molding us to help her achieve them. She was extremely concerned about what others would say and making sure that we wouldn't cause her any embarrassment, which led to hiding many things, including the fact that I was actually raised by my grandmother. Speaking openly about this matter provoked her disapproval, as she would reproach me for wanting to portray her as a bad mother and accuse me of harboring resentment towards her. Part of the obstacles in my relationship with my mother has been a lack of trust and expressions of love accompanied by one-way communication.

Every time I tried to open my heart and express my concerns to her or simply wanted to ask a question about my birth or childhood, it became a trigger, and she used defense mechanisms to avoid answering and discussing my history. I've never been interested in judging her, but I am interested in knowing the truth to understand and heal from many things that have affected me throughout my life. Culturally speaking, Hispanics face high pressure to present themselves as perfect and unapproachable parents. Often, the phrase "Respect me" is used as a shield to avoid difficult conversations, resolving relational problems, or setting healthy boundaries. I have learned that God teaches us to respect and love one another, to be a reflection of His love and mercy towards us. Perhaps you have seen in a medical appointment how the healthcare professional evaluates your symptoms to reach a conclusion, provide a diagnosis, and then treat the condition. The same goes for mental health. Just because multiple people are experiencing anxiety, trauma, and emotional pain doesn't mean they have all gone through the same situations; However, it is important to identify the emotional roots that lead to behavioral reactions affecting our relationships with others.

To provide further insight into my connections with other women who have experienced difficult relationships with their mothers, I will share some examples of behavioral patterns that have affected many individuals and hindered the establishment of a healthy emotional bond between mothers and daughters. Sons are not excluded from experiencing these types of relationships; However, My work has primarily focused on women who are healing from these relationships and working toward emotional and spiritual restoration.

TOXIC PATTERNS BETWEEN MOTHERS AND DAUGHTERS

1. **Authoritarian Mothers:** These mothers can be inflexible and stubborn when it comes to certain

expectations, emphasizing traditional gender roles. Statements like "I'm not raising you to marry someone who is below your social status," "A man should support you no matter the cost, that's his duty as a man," or "Going to university is useless if your role is to stay at home" are common. The authoritarian mother tends to react violently when she feels disregarded or disobeyed.

2. Dependent Mothers: In this relationship, it is the daughters who excessively care for their mothers, often starting from childhood. This damages the mother-daughter relationship as roles are reversed, leading to a dynamic where the daughter provides the care and support.

3. Controlling Mothers: These mothers have difficulty accepting and acknowledging their daughters' autonomy, not allowing them to make decisions or assert their own identity. This behavior leads to low self-esteem and insecurity in daughters.

4. Mothers with Ambivalent Bonds: Typically, these are passive-aggressive mothers in their communication style. Some days they are loving and considerate, while other days they are indifferent or cruel in their words. This type of treatment creates uncertainty, fear, and mistrust in daughters, as they never know who they will encounter when seeking their mother's presence.

5. Narcissistic Mothers: Based on my professional experience, I must admit that this is the most prevalent pattern in support group therapies. These mothers may view their daughters as extensions of themselves, projecting their own identity onto them. They want to shape their daughters' lives entirely based on their own perspective, without considering their daughters' opinions. This prevents the daughters from developing their own inner selves and frustrates them, leading to deep feelings of anxiety, depression, and damage to their self-esteem.

6. Mothers who employ belittling tactics: These mothers often make their daughters feel insignificant, constantly causing them to doubt their abilities and talents. This generates feelings of insecurity and fear when facing new challenges, with the false belief that everything they do is wrong. Statements like "You're good for nothing" or "You can't do anything right" become ingrained. The daughter becomes obsessed with trying to please her mother, knowing deep down that nothing she does will satisfy her, but still taking the risk of being mocked and belittled in the hope of gaining acceptance.

7. Invasive Mothers: In this mother-daughter relationship, healthy boundaries are usually non-existent, and when boundaries are set, they are not well received, resulting in conflict. The mother doesn't accept that her adult daughter can make decisions on her own without including her. Emotional manipulation tactics may be employed. This type of relationship affects trust and respect between the two parties.

8. Emotionally Distant Mothers: This relationship is characterized by a lack of affectionate displays, both emotionally and physically. There are no caresses, hugs, or even affectionate words or expressions of love, leading to an emotional disconnection that carries consequences into adulthood. These consequences can manifest as an inability to emotionally connect with others or, on the other extreme, excessive emotional dependency, seeking love to fill the emotional void.

It is important to identify these patterns in order to repair the bonds between parent and child and avoid repeating the same cycle in our relationships with our own children. I consider it crucial to spend individual time with our children, interacting with them based on their interests, personalities, and abilities. There are no perfect mothers, and we all make mistakes. In fact, I don't believe that anyone is perfect. However, I have learned that when we transform our mistakes and defeats into learning lessons, we can achieve success in any situation. My goal in explaining those years of my relationship with my mother is not to judge or blame her for how things have unfolded.

Our relationship continues to undergo changes, therapy, and counseling in order to establish healthy boundaries, deepen our understanding of each other, and comprehend the transformative power of God in our lives. With His guidance, we have come to realize that our past experiences were shaped by unresolved traumas that have reverberated through multiple generations. My mother, too, endured a traumatic childhood marred by paternal abandonment, maternal rejection, and emotional abuse, among other hardships. My sister and I, with God's unwavering support, have made a conscious choice to break free from these patterns of emotional suffering, make wiser decisions, and draw closer to Him. Through forgiveness and an earnest plea for God's love to envelop us, we strive to exhibit the same compassion and mercy that has been lavished upon us, transcending our former identities as orphans to embrace our true status as beloved daughters.

Today, I have an adult daughter, a teenager, and two young children. I take advantage of our routines when driving to school to ask them what worries them, what motivates them, and what they would like us to do together.

My son Joshua plays American football, and I confess that it's not a sport I know much about. I am still learning, so I've taken it upon myself to watch explanations on YouTube to have conversations with him and enjoy the games when I go to watch him play. I even bought a trivia card game about the history of American football and how it's played. Many times, it will be necessary for us to invest in our children's interests. During one of our outings for a meal, I felt a rush of joy as I witnessed his face light up with surprise upon hearing my words: "Can you explain to me the different roles of the players and the position you play?"

He started talking with great joy and enthusiasm, like a seasoned sports correspondent. I was amazed at how important this sport is in his life. Another one of Joshua's interests is wrestling, and he is a member of the school's wrestling team. I understand that sport much better because it's very popular in Nicaragua, and I always enjoyed attending wrestling events. My daughter Daniela is in university and she shares her goals and objectives with me. I have learned that listening to her is something that greatly helps us connect and grow our relationship. Daniela is assertive, and if something bothers her or makes her uncomfortable, she expresses it. I am grateful to God because I can see how He has been transforming our hearts and helping us to have a better relationship. I trust in God's promises and can find rest in knowing that everything that is yet to be resolved is in His hands and under His control. I believe that our hearts will be completely transformed, healed, and perfected by the One who was willing to give His life so that we could know the truth. Daniela is determined, hardworking, and focused on her tasks. She has always helped me with her siblings, but I have maintained the limit of not burdening her with too much responsibility for them. We have had tough moments during her adolescence, especially after witnessing her parents' divorce. God has guarded her heart, and something that has helped us greatly is speaking with truth, without judgment or reproach, while maintaining mutual respect. I have focused on not repeating what I have experienced with her. I have always reminded her that she can ask me questions about my life without fear, that there are difficult topics, but we can navigate them together. I have shown vulnerability, cried in front of her, and she has witnessed my processes and God's victories in my life.

My youngest son and I share a strong bond. Like many elementary school children, he is in the process of exploring his surroundings, discovering his abilities, and uncovering his interests. Mario firmly believes that it was God's choice for him to be an older brother, and his joy knew no bounds when he learned that his sister, Génesis, was on her way. He takes great pleasure in imparting his knowledge from church and school to her. Witnessing Génesis successfully carry out something he has taught her fills him with pure delight, and she, in turn, feels cherished by her siblings, as they all eagerly embrace the role of protectors and caregivers. Occasionally, I remind them that it's important to empower her to become independent. Despite her tender age, she has already grasped the closeness of her bond with her siblings and knows exactly whom to turn to when she requires assistance. Promoting unity among my children holds tremendous significance for me, as I believe it brings joy to God when siblings remain united and cherish their time together.

Due to the closeness in age, I can see that unity in Mario and Génesis, and my heart is filled with joy when I see them, which helps me understand what God expects from me in my relationship with my sister and with other people. I take refuge in God's promises, and I can rest knowing that everything that is yet to be resolved is in His hands and under His control. I trust that our hearts will be completely transformed, healed, and perfected by the One who was willing to give His life so that we could experience the love of the Father in our lives. Jesus has triumphed over every barrier that once separated us from God the Father. As a result, we now enjoy direct access to Him and can place our complete trust in His care. I vividly recall the moment when my rebellious heart found solace in the embrace of my Father, the day I surrendered my orphanhood, and He whispered to my heart, "I have called you by name, you are mine" (Isaiah 43:1). Shortly thereafter, my beloved sister, whom I love dearly. brought me a gift adorned with that very same verse. It served as a divine confirmation from my Father, assuring me that I am His beloved daughter and that a new life had commenced.

Within His sacred Scriptures, God promises that He will reconcile the hearts of fathers with their children and guide the wayward souls onto the path of righteousness, all in preparation of a people willing to embrace His purpose (Luke 1:17).

CHAPTER 5
IDENTITY

Personal identity encompasses a collection of distinct traits that characterize an individual, including attitudes, talents, abilities, character, temperament, virtues, faith, and self-concept. These elements enable us to distinguish ourselves from others and recognize our unique individuality and personality.

Childhood and adolescent traumas leave a lasting impact on individuals throughout their lives. According to the National Institute of Mental Health, traumas are defined as emotionally distressing events that a person experiences, often originating in childhood. These traumas can result in enduring mental and physical effects, some of which manifest in our emotions and relationships. An adult's identity is often deeply influenced by their self-concept, which can be shaped by traumas and circumstances encountered during earlier developmental stages before reaching adulthood. In this chapter, we delve into how the experiences we have undergone shape and mold our character and personality, which serve as vital components of our identity. We explore both our social identity and our identity in God, with the latter being the key to renewing our minds. By embracing our identity as God's children, we define ourselves not by material possessions or societal expectations but by the promises He has bestowed upon our lives. We believe that God has a divine plan for us and will guide us throughout our journey of self-discovery, providing unwavering support until our transformation is complete.

The concept of identity traces its origins back to the research conducted by the American-German psychoanalyst Erik H. Erikson (1902-1994). Erikson defined identity as the integration of various aspects of an individual's self.

The formation of identity is a pivotal aspect of human development. Erikson posited that adolescence is a period during which significant milestones contribute to the construction of one's self. It is a phase characterized by personality development, where ideas are chosen and shaped, ultimately becoming integral components of our personality and identity. Adolescence serves as a stage in which we define ourselves, embracing, accepting, and expressing our support or opposition to various ideas and values.

Young individuals begin to comprehend commitments, responsibilities, and envision a future for their lives. They embark on the journey of seeking employment, affirming or rejecting religious beliefs, forging friendships, entering romantic relationships, and determining their place within the family, society, politics, and the church.

The development of a weak self, devoid of emotional support and roots, hinders the ability to establish healthy and positive relationships in adulthood.

Many young people lose hope when they see that their current situation limits them from envisioning goals and dreams. They feel disadvantaged compared to peers who have both parents at home or enjoy a social position that grants them more privileges and opportunities. These young individuals may experience depression and anxiety as their dreams, goals, and objectives appear impossible to achieve within their current reality.

When I worked in the west side of San Antonio, I observed that while not all social factors have been established, the following situations greatly influence adolescents and can lead them from optimism to pessimism: parents going through divorce, pending cases in juvenile court, a household where the mother is solely responsible for all expenses and is the only one working, economic difficulties, lack of emotional support, and lack of participation in sports and recreational activities. I have seen that these circumstances contribute to mental health disorders in children and adolescents that are more common than we think. To give us an idea, research conducted by the National Alliance on Mental Illness (NAMI) reveals that 50% of all lifelong mental illnesses begin by the age of 14, and 75% by the age of 24. Depression, anxiety, and other mental health conditions can have different origins, but the alarming and increasing numbers demonstrate that there are several factors—some of which have been mentioned earlier—that we must monitor in our adolescents. It is of utmost importance to observe family dynamics and implement educational programs that can help our young people and their families in various areas of their needs.

HUMAN NEEDS: MASLOW'S HIERARCHY

Maslow's hierarchy is a theory that defines the structure of human needs. Abraham Maslow created a pyramid to illustrate the sequential order of these needs, organizing them as follows:

1. **Physiological needs:** Shelter, clothing, hygiene, medication, and assurance of survival.

2. **Safety needs:** People have the need to feel protected from physical and emotional harm, among others.

3. **Social needs:** The need to be accepted, loved, to interact with others, and to be recognized as individuals. The need for a sense of belonging is especially important in this category.

4. **Need for recognition:** People have the need for their work and contributions to be acknowledged. This leads individuals to develop self-respect, self-confidence, and autonomy.

5. **Self-actualization needs:** The pinnacle of Maslow's pyramid and often the most sought-after level to achieve.

These encompass the needs for personal growth and the fulfillment of one's potential. Individuals strive to develop themselves fully, utilizing their knowledge and skills. They aspire to accomplish both personal and professional goals, embracing opportunities for self-expression, being heard, and unleashing their creativity.

Maslow's Hierarchy is a starting point used to develop successful interventions, and I have personally used it and witnessed the impact it has, especially when young people learn to fulfill the need for love. That is why I would place the need to know God as the number one need, as knowing God's love leads us to feel loved, accepted, and a sense of belonging as children of God. There is a great opportunity to impact the identity of many young people when community centers with missions, visions, and values established in Christ come together to meet immediate needs while also providing emotional and spiritual support to young people seeking love, acceptance, and guidance. Jesus showed us on many occasions that spiritual provision precedes physical provision—as seen in the miracle of the five thousand (Matthew 14:13-21)—and He also reminds us that nothing is impossible for Him. When the needs in Maslow's hierarchy are left unfulfilled, desperation and a lack of hope can arise. Each follower of Jesus is called to help others, work in unity, and be a light in the darkness. This includes the lives of those going through difficulties.

Jesus teaches us the profound truth that we can navigate life with unwavering faith, trusting in what is unseen. There are moments when we may relate to the young man in the story, possessing only a meager offering of a few fish and loaves of bread. In those moments, we might be tempted to believe that our resources are insufficient to meet the needs before us. However, I want to assure you that when we choose to believe, extraordinary possibilities unfold.

Within our community, we have embarked on initiatives that have made a tangible difference in the lives of families. Through collaboration, sponsorship from local supermarkets and small businesses, we have been able to provide essential items to those in need. Additionally, we have established community closets where individuals of all ages can freely select what they require, pantries specifically tailored for university students, and extended emotional and financial support to single parents. Our collective efforts encompass community collaboration, as various ministries unite to deliver supplies and other essentials to those facing adversity. It is during these outreach endeavors that we seize the opportunity to nourish spirits and bring forth a transformative encounter with God for all who embrace a new identity in Him.

Through our journey, we can discover that the Creator of all things holds the keys to our destiny, and with His victorious hand guiding us, all things become possible. I have personally witnessed the profound transformation of young individuals as they embrace new mindsets, realizing that their origin does not determine their destiny. With God by their side, they begin to grasp that no goal is insurmountable and dreams can indeed be realized. In the realm of Christian counseling, many young people are introduced to the life of Jesus during His youth, unveiling His close relationship with the Heavenly Father. This revelation serves as a powerful reminder of the unwavering closeness we can experience with God. Jesus, unlike us, did not need to develop a super ego or a strong sense of self. He possessed a resolute identity rooted in the Great I Am and maintained unwavering communication with Him. This profound connection fostered guidance, protection, and provision, enabling Jesus to fulfill His purpose and live a life on earth that brought pleasure to the Father's eyes. Indeed, God Himself testified to this truth, proclaiming, "This is my beloved Son, in whom I am well pleased" (Matthew 3:17). There is a great transformation that is evident when we teach our youth to follow the direction and example of Jesus, who has given us all the benefits of love and the grace of the Father through His sacrifice for all of us.

CHARACTER, TEMPERAMENT AND DISCIPLINE

To develop our identity in the different stages of our lives, it is important to understand that character plays a significant role. However, character should not be confused with temperament. Character encompasses a combination of traits, qualities, and circumstances that reflect a person's nature and way of thinking. It contributes to defining our identity within various groups or stages we experience. Temperament and character are distinct terms. You may have heard the expression, "They easily get angry; they have a strong character." In reality, this does not signify a strong character, but rather a temperament that is easily provoked to anger or rage by emotional triggers.

Learning and modifying character qualities is a stepping stone toward encountering our true selves, guided by plans and purposes aligned with God's original design for our lives. Once we identify areas that require transformation, discipline and focus are necessary to achieve the desired change. The objective is not to discover who we are in order to be superior to others, but to truly find ourselves and transform destructive behaviors, habits, and emotions that hinder our progress and growth toward a better version according to God's plan. Throughout this process, our concept of ourselves evolves, as God's concept remains steadfast. The skills and talents you possess are integral to His plan. By sharing our personal narratives, we assist others in embarking on a journey towards becoming new individuals, fully embracing God's identity in our lives, souls, and hearts.

Discovering your interests will lead you to complete projects and approach them with responsibility, discipline, and dedication, taking control of your decisions and understanding that they will have consequences that will either bring you closer to your goals or steer you away from them. We achieve a firm identity when we can live without blaming others. We no longer remain trapped in decisions made by others on our behalf.

Finding your identity reveals that you may have experienced circumstances beyond your control. However, as a survivor of traumatic events, you have reached a point where you no longer depend on others' decisions to navigate your life. Instead, you rely solely on the care and guidance of the Father to reshape your story and achieve emotional healing. The key lies in discovering yourself and, above all, having an intimate encounter with your Heavenly Father.

The Word of God serves as a transformative tool, challenging and correcting any misconceptions or false beliefs we may hold about ourselves. Our identity can be significantly influenced by our physical appearance, special needs, or limitations resulting from temporary or permanent disabilities. Young people, particularly, are highly conscious of their physical appearance and may assign excessive importance to their own looks and the judgments of others. In support groups, a popular verse among young individuals is 2 Timothy 1:7, which reminds us that beyond the fear of non-acceptance or criticism due to limitations or disabilities, we possess the power of the Spirit of God. This power empowers us to strive, be courageous, and have mastery over our minds, focusing on the things that truly matter.

"For God has not given us a spirit of fear and timidity, but of power, love, and self-discipline."
2 Timothy 1:7 (NLT)

In God's original plan, He gave us the will and power to choose a spirit without fear, a spirit that can be filled with His love and provides us with the ability for self-control, which is highly necessary for managing our emotions. The apostle Paul writes to the young preacher Timothy, addressing him as a spiritual son and speaking to him as a mentor in his letters. Paul makes sure to advise him in all areas and reminds him that his youth is not an obstacle to serving God. Paul mentions various aspects of his life, starting by commenting on the respect and admiration he has for Timothy's grandmother and mother, who instilled in him a love for God and biblical teachings. Paul doesn't mention a father at home; we don't know the reasons.

However, he repeatedly reminds Timothy that he has support, counsel, and guidance from him to overcome any obstacles he may face in his personal and ministerial life. When we listen to good advice and learn self-control and self-mastery, we become responsible individuals for our own future and for the sake of those we love. God does not invite us to worry about the future; He invites us to trust in Him, knowing that He is preparing good plans for our lives. God has a future and an eternal purpose for which we were created.

Discovering that we are loved by God—a Father who not only longed for us before we were born but also created us with love and care—helps us build a new identity as His children. I enjoy sharing with parents that in the eyes of our children, we are people of great influence. We always have a ready audience to imprint on their memories our qualities, mistakes, examples, conversations, and our determination to be emotionally stable individuals with the help of God. Our children, even though it may not always seem so, are aware of the examples of faith they see in us and the importance we place on our relationship with our Heavenly Father. God loves His creation and desires a relationship with His children.

OUR IDENTITY IN GOD AS HIS CREATION

God has known us since before the foundation of the world (Ephesians 1:4). You and I have been created in His image and likeness. I often ponder how meticulously God fashioned every aspect of our being, considering both the physical and spiritual dimensions. At the very moment of our creation, God bestowed upon us our primary identity:

the identity of being part of His magnificent creation. The Creator of all things dedicated special care and attention to fashion each one of us with distinctive characteristics. He showered us with gifts that can never be taken away, delighting in us just as a father eagerly anticipates the arrival of his newborn child. Recognizing the importance of companionship, God sought to provide Adam with a partner, realizing it was not good for him to be alone. With equal love and tenderness, God created women to stand alongside men. Every intricate detail of our existence, crafted in His image and likeness, serves a purpose that was established from the beginning. Our Father's love for us has been unwavering since our inception. While everything God created was good, it was when He formed the human being that He declared it "very good," akin to the fulfillment a father experiences upon witnessing his children take their first breaths. I vividly recall the anticipation my husband and I felt as we waited in the maternity section of the hospital, eagerly preparing to welcome our first child into the world. I can still see the longing and joy in my husband's eyes as he gazed at the crib we would use to welcome our baby into the delivery room; the joy in his heart was reflected on his face.

Our identity is given to us by God. We are made in His image, resembling the Creator of the universe. In the Garden of Eden, Adam and Eve had a well-established relationship with their Creator. Our relationship with God is key to developing our identity. We are all born with an identity obscured by sin, but God longs to restore us to have a relationship with Him and guide us towards a new identity that resembles Him. People tend to create groups with similar characteristics that involve traits, stories, and factors that define them, such as origin, nationality, race, culture, and beliefs that they take on as part of their identity. Many times, we can see the struggle for acceptance within one group or another, and divisions based on social class and racial or ethnic background. King Solomon observed these social phenomena and noted them in his writings in the book of Proverbs, coming to one conclusion that is summarized in this verse: "The rich and the poor have this in common: The LORD is the Maker of them all." Proverbs 22:2 (NIV)

In our society, we can see that when someone enjoys a high financial position, their origin, nationality, and race become irrelevant because we are swayed by their credit score and their wealth reduced to their purchasing power. With wealth, friends increase, but even a friend of the poor may abandon them (Proverbs 19:4 NIV). Jesus reminded us on many occasions that our identity should not be rooted in wealth; both the rich and the poor will have the same end. Jesus had followers who financially supported His ministry, but their identity was not in what they possessed but in the impact they could make using their resources.

IF GOD KNEW THAT WE WOULD FAIL, WHY DID HE CREATE US?

God knows all things, and He chose to create us out of love. When humans decide to have children or adopt them, there is no guarantee that the love they give will be reciprocated. Some fear not being good parents or not being able to receive love. However, God teaches us that in love, there is no fear; perfect love drives out fear. The one who fears is not perfected in love (1 John 4:18). God's love compels us to love our children without expecting anything in return, to dedicate our time, strength, and efforts to provide them with opportunities. In many Bible studies, I have been asked this question: "If God knew we would fail, then why did He create us?" God has placed an answer to this question in my heart, and I know it comes from His wisdom. God does not delight in being loved or obeyed by force; by giving us free will, He has bestowed upon us a great gift of His love. The choice between good and evil, obedience and disobedience, has always existed since the Garden of Eden.

Teaching our children about God's identity and love equips them with the tools to avoid falling into the deception of a false identity, one that is distant from God. Satan, too, was created with free will, and the Bible describes the care and love with which God created him in Ezekiel 28:11-19. Through a comparison with the king of Tyre, God speaks about how the heart can become filled with pride and how creation can rebel, exalting itself and believing that the Creator of all can be replaced and dethroned from our lives. We can allow our pride and arrogance to reign, leading to a complete separation from God, not only in this physical life but also for eternity Deciding to let ourselves be consumed by pride and complete self-reliance only allows for us to remain solely as creations without purpose, direction, and a relationship with the Father. The deceiver who succeeded in Eden accomplished his purpose with Adam and Eve; However, he did not achieve his purpose with Jesus, the Son of God.

IDENTITY AS ORPHANS

"The thief comes only to steal, kill, and destroy. I have come that they may have life, and have it to the full."
John 10:10

In Eden, the thief stole our home, our provisions, and above all, he stole our walk with God. He took away the

Father who used to walk and talk with His children every evening. He left us orphaned without mercy or compassion. He fed Eve lie after lie, making her doubt the word of her Father. And he left Adam inactive and lifeless, unable to speak or take action, just like the bite of a snake.

Some elderly people have fallen victim to well-planned scams. Thieves exploit their lack of technological knowledge, just as the enemy seized the perfect moment to deceive us, knowing that we would lose the greatest gift we could have: our home alongside the Father. Because of disobedience and trusting the father of lies, we became orphans without direction or support, constantly on the defensive, ready to fight for survival. We wear masks to protect ourselves and lie to hide our history, driven by shame, guilt, and the burden of inherited sin in this fallen world. Even when we fell for the deception, God, in His immense love and mercy, devised a plan to protect and save us for eternity, so that we could once again hear His voice. He rescued us from orphanhood and restored us as His children through Jesus' sacrifice for our sins. Jesus truly came to restore all that had been stolen from us.

The book "The Case for Grace," written by Lee Strobel, tells the story of a young girl from South Korea who was born after the war and was thrown out of her home at the age of four. She learned to survive on her own, enduring unimaginable hardships, suffering sexual exploitation, and enduring physical abuse from people on the streets due to not being fully Korean. She was born to a union between an American soldier and a Korean mother. A nurse decided to take her to an orphanage, where she was considered too old to be adopted, but they provided her with food and shelter. Eventually, an American couple saw her and made the decision to adopt her. Initially, she didn't know how to accept love, and when the man who wanted to be her father showed her affection, she reacted by spitting at him and running away.

However, despite this, the couple chose to adopt her and bring her into their home. The young girl initially believed she was going to be a servant, but the couple showed her love and mercy, ultimately saving her in many ways. It was through this adoption that the young girl finally discovered her true identity when a neighbor told her that she was their daughter. This example serves as an illustration of what happens to a believer. In Romans 8:15-16, it explains that we have been adopted into God's family, and we can rejoice and declare with fullness, "We are His children!"

As believers, we can choose to cling to the identity of orphans, or we can embrace the love of our Heavenly Father and assume a new identity as sons and daughters. The bridge that leads us from orphanhood to being children is found in Christ. We cannot receive the immediate inheritance of salvation unless we first accept Jesus as our Lord and Savior, acknowledging our sins in this wicked world and confessing Jesus with our mouths. Through this acceptance, we are gifted with the Holy Spirit, enabling us to hear the voice of our Father and be guided by Him to receive His blessings, love, grace, and goodness throughout our journey in life.

When I began my walk with Christ, I had a deep longing to hear the voice of my Heavenly Father. I immersed myself in the Word of the Lord, studying and praying to receive His Holy Spirit. I came across a book about the Holy Spirit and decided to engage in one of the prayer exercises recommended in the book to learn how to pray. The exercise required me to remain still and silent, not uttering a word. After forty minutes had passed, my thoughts became distracting, leading me to anticipate what the Father was going to say to me. Numerous things crossed my mind until suddenly, a great peace and stillness settled within me, and I heard the words, "I love you, my daughter." Joy surged through my heart, and it was a remarkable experience to hear my Heavenly Father speak to me about His love. On that day, I was filled with happiness because I realized that I had transitioned from being an orphan to being a beloved daughter.

IDENTITY OF THE CHILDREN

In adulthood, our identity is influenced by various aspects of our lives: being single, the changes brought by marital status through marriage or divorce, the profession or occupation we choose, our relationships with different groups of people, and our faith. Currently, the United States is undergoing an identity crisis, a period characterized by profound doubts. These doubts lead individuals to question the meaning of their existence, often accompanied by feelings of emptiness and loneliness. When discussing this crisis, I am not referring to social preferences or definitions that can vary among individuals. Rather, I am referring to the lack of love, guidance, order, and purpose that has tragically led many people to contemplate suicide.

A person's identity as a child is directly linked to their relationship with their father. The U.S. census reveals that 18.4 million children (1 in 4) are living without their biological father, adoptive father, or stepfather in their homes. Research studies consistently confirm that the absence of a father negatively impacts the development of a child's identity. Conversely, the presence of fathers has a positive impact on the lives of mothers and their children.

National Fatherhood is an organization dedicated to raising awareness about the importance of fathers in the family, the need to prioritize children even in the face of changing family structures, and providing support to fathers and mothers to enable them to care for their families effectively. National Fatherhood focuses on eight key aspects, but three of them particularly caught my attention:

1. **The societal cost of an absent father:** Fathers may be absent from their children's lives due to various reasons, including incarceration, divorce, abandonment, custody issues, or limited visitation enforced by the children's mother. While some of these limitations are valid due to safety concerns, there are instances where the mother's new partner prevents the father from maintaining a close relationship with their children, causing significant emotional harm and often jeopardizing the children's physical safety. The presence of fathers in their children's lives reduces the occurrence of emotional problems, enhances academic performance, lowers the likelihood of incarceration, and minimizes or prevents alcohol and substance use.

2. **Children's sense of security, protection, and love amidst sudden life changes:** Shared parenting, numerous research studies demonstrate that shared parenting yields lifelong benefits for our children. One of the most significant advantages is its positive influence on attachment security by establishing strong relationships between both parents.

Co-parenting refers to the mutual support between two individuals who share the common goal of ensuring the well-being of their children, regardless of whether they are a couple, their compatibility, or their current relationship status. Caregivers' attitudes and relationships play a vital role in a child or adolescent's life, and co-parenting involves parents reaching a mutual agreement on how to meet their children's physical, emotional, and spiritual needs in terms of support, protection, and development.

3. Impact on women's well-being: Mothers experience numerous benefits when fathers are actively involved in pregnancy and child-rearing. Women are more likely to receive prenatal care, less likely to smoke during pregnancy, have a lower risk of postpartum depression, experience less parenting-related stress, and have more free time to spend with their partners, socialize, pursue education, and engage in self-care.

The absence of fathers in their children's lives can be prevented, cycles can be broken, and relationships can be established, as long as it is feasible and in the best interest of the children. While reviewing various statistics, research studies, and relevant literature is essential to educate ourselves about this issue, I believe it is of utmost importance to educate adults, young people, and teenage parents to prevent the repetition of negative attitudes and behaviors. We must teach them that they have the power to break the cycle and eliminate detrimental patterns that have been passed down from generation to generation, adversely impacting their lives. By doing so, we can help them discover their true identity as beloved children and enable them to be filled with God's love, allowing them to love their own children.

It is crucial to explain the significant dangers associated with father absence in children's lives, as it exposes them to a fourfold higher risk of living in poverty, behavioral problems, infant mortality, an increased likelihood of incarceration, and a higher probability of experiencing abuse or neglect. Additionally, the likelihood of dropping out of school doubles, and for young girls, the chances of teenage pregnancy are seven times higher. Our children need to be equipped with the truth. Although they will encounter difficulties in life, God's love as a Father will be present in each of these challenges.

"Listen, my son, to your father's instruction and do not forsake your mother's teaching. They are a garland to grace your head and a chain to adorn your neck." (Proverbs 1:8-9)

Jesus chose to obey the Father and remain in Him, and through His obedience, He obtained the victory that grants us the freedom we had lost. We were all condemned to endless cycles of abandonment and rejection, separated from our Father. Let us remember that Jesus has set us free, and His perfect love casts out our fears and the experiences that have hindered the formation of our identity. When we come to the feet of Jesus, we may still grapple with challenges and face the realities of our fallen humanity. However, this does not mean that we are unworthy, unforgiven, or unaccepted. In Christ, we are imperfect yet loved sons and daughters of a perfect God.

IDENTITY IN GOD

I would like to clarify that identity in God is not about perfection. It is not a checklist of things we can or cannot do, and it is not a religion. Identity in God is the restoration of the spiritual DNA that the Father planned for us from the beginning. It is an identity rooted in His perfect plan for His children, and it also involves receiving His Spirit. As new believers, we often expect an immediate and complete transformation. While Jesus can certainly set you free and bring instant healing on many occasions, certain habits, beliefs, fears, or other aspects may persist, which God allows for gradual processing, spiritual growth, and the shaping of His finished work in us.

This new identity allows us to be born again. When we are filled with God's identity, our desires align with His. We start making decisions that please Him, even if they may displease others. We become deeply convicted to do what is right. We make changes in our lives willingly, leaving behind the past, the pain, the emptiness, and everything that kept us tied to an identity that did not align with God's plan for our lives. We view the struggles of others without judgment, extending the same mercy we have received. We recognize that we are all on the journey of life, and despite negative circumstances, God is always present, equipping us with the tools to overcome obstacles, hardships, and unexpected situations.

The identity of the kingdom of God is not based on wealth, even though this world may appear to be dominated by it. Superficially, it may seem that racial and social diversity, struggles for gender equality, and other social causes are the root issues in this world. However, in my opinion, everything ultimately boils down to whether or not one has money. We can observe that a person considered part of a racial minority may encounter opportunities if they are wealthy, while another person from the same racial group may face closed doors if they are not millionaires. The true domination on Earth is not based on races, social status, or royal lineage, but rather on wealth. Jesus continually reminds us that wealth cannot be a god in our lives and that our identity cannot be rooted and grounded solely in the money we possess or desire to possess. Identity in God transcends earthly possessions. It directs our focus towards heavenly matters rather than material wealth. God loves us and has wonderful promises for His children.

In this list, you will find what God says about our identity:

- We are loved by God (John 15:9).
- We are children of God (John 1:12).
- Chosen by Christ (Ephesians 1:4).
- Sanctified by the truth (John 17:17).
- Justified by faith (Romans 5:1).
- Redeemed and forgiven of all our sins (Colossians 1:14).
- Servants of righteousness (Romans 6:18).
- Heirs of God (Galatians 4:6-7).
- We are children of light, not darkness (1 Thessalonians 5:5).
- Citizens of heaven (Philippians 3:20).
- Pilgrims in this world (1 Peter 2:11).
- We are ministers of reconciliation (2 Corinthians 5:18-19).
- We are friends of Christ (John 15:15).
- Protected by God (1 John 5:18).

- We are the temple of the Holy Spirit (1 Corinthians 3:16).
- Chosen before the foundation of the world (Ephesians 1:4).
- We are a new creation (2 Corinthians 5:17).
- We are free from condemnation (Romans 8:1).
- We have been created for good works (Ephesians 2:10).
- Covered by God (Hebrews 13:5).
- Strengthened by the power of the Holy Spirit (Ephesians 3:16).

Jesus confidently, firmly, and diligently shared that He had been sent by the Heavenly Father. He was unwavering in His identity in the Father, even in the face of mockery, criticism, and suffering for being called the Son of God. He never lost sight of the mission God had entrusted Him with—to share the good news so that we too could come to know the Father and follow the path that leads us back home. Jesus taught us the power of communication through prayer and assured us that the Father listens to our requests, prepares a place for us to be with Him for eternity, and has already shown us the way to reach that destination.

In this chapter, I desire to offer you a prayer that will assist you on your journey to embrace a new identity in Christ. Remember, His Spirit will accompany you in every step, gradually perfecting you until the work is complete. As a teacher, He has a beautiful plan for your life and the lives of your descendants.

"Jesus said to him, 'I am the way, and the truth, and the life. No one comes to the Father except through me.'"
(John 14:6)

PRAYER:

Beloved Heavenly Father, I humbly acknowledge my sins. I recognize that I have allowed my past to shape my identity and have strayed from You by forgetting Your Word, Your purpose for my life, and the precious gift that Christ has prepared for me through His sacrificial cleansing of my sins. From the depths of my heart, I confess that Christ has risen and is gloriously alive. Today, I choose to return home, Father. I know that there will be rejoicing in heaven because today I decide to surrender my life and my heart into Your loving hands.

Father, I pray that You take full control of my life and guide me according to Your perfect plan for me as Your beloved child. Fill my heart with boundless love for others and grant me intimate knowledge of You. Fill every void within me, enabling me to forgive, experience true freedom, and live a life that testifies to Your faithfulness, love, and grace. I commit to walking with You until the end. I thank You and rest in Your promises, in the name of Jesus. Amen.

CHAPTER 6
A FATHER AFTER GOD'S OWN HEART

As I work in the community, I have witnessed the crucial need for a father figure in the lives of children and adolescents. I must confess that I used to hold the belief that a mother's love would suffice for her children, and that they wouldn't require a father's love. However, I now understand that this is far from the truth. The love of both parents is profoundly significant for the development and growth of children. While a mother can provide immense love and care, she cannot offer the unique love of a father. The mother is wonderfully designed for the role of motherhood, not fatherhood.

In situations where children lack a father figure, the mother can demonstrate God's love and teach them about the fatherhood of God. The Heavenly Father possesses the power to fill the voids that arise in the lives of children, voids that can detrimentally impact their self-esteem and future relationships with others. I acknowledge that biological parents may not always be willing or able to participate in the upbringing of their children or be present in their lives. It is also essential to recognize that it may not always be safe to maintain a relationship with a father who has inflicted physical, mental, and emotional abuse upon their children.

Moreover, I want to emphasize that I do not aim to portray single mothers in a negative light. My own mother was a single mother, and I experienced single parenthood myself for a period of time. I comprehend the countless efforts and sacrifices they make within circumstances beyond their control. My intention is to shed light on a need that I personally experienced due to the absence of a relationship with my father, influenced by factors beyond my control and my own decisions at one point. Throughout my adolescence, I grappled with an immense void, and as an adult, I witnessed the emotional and spiritual healing that my Heavenly Father's fatherhood brought into my life. God has made me feel loved and protected. I have shared my testimony of encountering the Heavenly Father and observed how young individuals who have grown up without their parents or are involved in state programs relate to my experience, open their hearts, and begin the process of filling those voids with God's love.

Instead of seeking solace in temporary pursuits, substance abuse, sexual promiscuity, or toxic relationships in search of love, I advocate for focusing on the substantial transformation that comes from embracing God's love. I had a profoundly meaningful experience when I was appointed as the director of a program called Puente, which provided child care assistance for parents who were working or pursuing education. To my pleasant surprise, during the first semester, the majority of participants were single fathers with children under the age of five. As part of the program, we conducted weekly meetings to assess if there were any needs we could address at the community center. Through these conversations, I discovered that many of these fathers had daughters, and they faced challenges regarding toilet training and using public restrooms when they were alone with their girls. At that time, certain groups were advocating for inclusive restrooms in the state of Texas. However, this proposal failed to address the specific need within our community. It became apparent during these interviews that we had not been attentive to the needs of single fathers.

As social workers, we seize these opportunities when people are pushing for legislation in various areas to advocate for the needs we see in our cities, organizations, and community centers, and to raise awareness of the issues affecting vulnerable populations in great need of support. My intention was not to create divisions about who needed a restroom more, but rather to shed light on the needs of single fathers. That year, with the help of letters, emails, calls to representatives, and many prayers from the community, family restrooms were incorporated into shopping centers and some public places.

Perhaps there are numerous unaddressed needs in your community that demand the intervention of someone or a collective to offer support like in the aforementioned case where a select few fathers had been awarded custody of their sons and daughters, and encountered distinctive challenges specific to their situation.

During my tenure at the Domestic Relations Office in Bexar County, I had the opportunity to engage with numerous fathers who were actively seeking to assume responsibility for their children. However, they encountered a myriad of hurdles that proved insurmountable without the assistance of a legal team and the observations of a social worker. These dedicated professionals had the arduous task of compiling comprehensive reports and providing testimonies in court based on their assessments derived from home studies or social evaluations.

Accompanied by my supervisor, I would visit single fathers, and it was heartening to witness the relief that washed over their faces upon discovering that their assigned social worker was a fellow man. Some fathers openly expressed their concerns about potential bias from female social workers, as they perceived a systemic inclination towards granting full custody to mothers at the expense of fathers' rights. Thankfully, in recent years, significant reforms have been implemented in the field of custody evaluation, prioritizing the well-being of children over traditional or cultural norms. Technology has played a pivotal role in promoting child welfare, facilitating the creation of blogs, websites, and signature campaigns aimed at addressing the issues, situations, and obstacles that impact families.

The population of single fathers has been steadily increasing. The most recent data from the US census (2020) revealed that 30% of children nationwide reside in households headed by a single parent. According to a study conducted by Child Trends, the primary contributing factors to this phenomenon are high divorce rates and the prevalence of children born outside of marriage. In 2019, the Pew Research Center confirmed that the United States possesses the highest number of children living in single-parent households compared to other countries. These statistics show the significance of recognizing and addressing the distinct challenges confronted by single fathers, as well as the imperative for robust support systems that empower them to fulfill their parental roles with efficacy.

These responses from fathers I have interviewed over

the years during different processes highlight the diverse experiences and emotions they go through. It is evident that being a single father or going through a divorce presents unique challenges and complexities. However, it is crucial to recognize that the bond between parents and their children continues even after separation or divorce. While couples may choose to distance themselves, they will always share a connection through their children and, later on, grandchildren, as I witnessed with my own parents. Grandchildren eventually became the link that facilitated communication.

NOW, I WILL SHARE WITH YOU A FEW MORE RESPONSES FROM FATHERS I HAVE INTERVIEWED THROUGHOUT THE YEARS:

- **Single father:** "It's challenging to take care of her, but she is my world. And even though I sometimes feel lonely, I believe it's better this way for now. I've been on a few dates, but I'm not ready to leave her with people I barely know. I didn't have a father, and she needs me. My mom helps me take care of her. My daughter and I are very close."

- **Divorced father:** "I wish I could have them with me more often, but we have a 50/50 custody agreement. Sometimes, it bothers me that my kids don't want me to discipline them. I feel like they see the time they spend with me as purely for fun, but I want them to learn responsibilities too."

- **Teenage father:** "I'm eighteen, and so is my girlfriend. We have a baby, and my parents help us out. I study and work, but sometimes, it's not enough. I tell them that there are moments when I feel overwhelmed, and I'm not sure if I'm doing the right thing. My parents support me a lot, but I feel the pressure to be a good father and provide for my child."

These firsthand accounts reflect the varying circumstances and perspectives of single fathers and divorced fathers, emphasizing the emotional complexities they navigate while striving to fulfill their parental roles. It is essential to acknowledge their experiences and provide support and resources to help them overcome the unique challenges they face.

- **Incarcerated father:** "It hurts not being able to be part of their activities. The internet helps us now. I know they wish I could be there with them. It saddens me that they have to pay the consequences of my mistakes. Here, I've grown closer to God, and I pray for Him to protect and guide them to become good people, to study, and to make something of themselves in life."

- **Military father:** "I miss my family. One thing I don't like when I come back home is that sometimes it's not well-received when I try to discipline my children. It's as if I've been away, and now I'm coming to scold them; it's like I've lost authority."

- **Immigrant father:** "You know, sometimes I'm tired. I miss my family, and I want to have a video call where I don't hear about all the bills to pay or problems to solve right away. I also want to hear that I'm loved, that I'm missed. It's embarrassing to share this because men are not supposed to talk about emotions, but that's how I feel."

- **Adoptive father:** "My brother passed away when my

nephew was two years old, and I've taken care of him ever since. I pray to God that he never lacks assistance for his schooling and his plans. He has been a great son, a gift from God in my life. I don't see him as my nephew; I see him as my own child, and he sees me as his dad."

- **Paternal grandfather:** "My son died in the war, and I've taken on the responsibility of caring for his children. I pray to God for good health so that I can take care of them and be there for them."

These accounts from fathers in different circumstances illustrate the unique challenges they face and the deep emotional connections they have with their children. Whether it's a single father, a divorced father, an incarcerated father, a military father, an immigrant father, an adoptive father, or a paternal grandfather, each one expresses their experiences and the profound love they have for their children. It is crucial to recognize and support fathers in their roles as they navigate various life situations and strive to provide the best for their kids.

- **Father with special physical mobility needs:** "I try to be present in everything I can. Sometimes my health doesn't allow it due to medical routines, but if it's possible, I'll be there for my children. God helps me overcome the obstacles of each day and gives me the strength to carry on. My desire is for them to grow close to God and become good men and women. The most important thing to me is that they make progress by applying what I've taught them in their lives. They are my arrows, and God takes care of them because He is faithful."

I am grateful to the fathers who shared their experiences with me during my journey as a social worker in the communities of San Antonio. I have seen these fathers overcome obstacles alongside their sons and daughters, reunite with their families, establish small businesses, and provide for their children while always being present in their lives.

Like many children, I also cherish the moments I shared with my father and learned many things from him. As I mentioned before, my father was not a man of many words, but when he gave advice, it was taken to heart because it usually came with a hint of experience, something he had lived through. When I started communicating with my father more frequently, my focus was not on what he had done right or wrong, but to make up for the time we didn't have together. God was very good to me by allowing me to be with him during the last months of his life.

I keep my father's graduation ring from law school in my office. He told me that he completed his law degree a year before I was born and shared the sacrifices he and my mother made for him to complete his studies. My father saw my mother as a hardworking and diligent woman, but he deeply regretted that unresolved traumas, both his and hers, filled their hearts with pride, bitterness, resentment, and mistrust. My father acknowledged the harm he had caused to my mother and his family; He acknowledged it, and God granted him forgiveness and mercy before calling him into His presence. Forgiving our earthly father leads us to resemble our Heavenly Father more, who places in our hearts the ability to forgive in order to receive forgiveness. If we refuse to forgive those who offend us, our hearts become closed and insensitive to the voice of our Heavenly Father. By confessing our lack of forgiveness and expressing our true emotions to God, we surrender our will to Him, allowing Him to assist us in dealing with those feelings. As we confess our sins, He remains faithful and just, forgiving our sins and purifying us from all unrighteousness. If we harbor hatred and resentment in our hearts, denying its presence, we deceive ourselves and reject the truth of God's Word. But if we acknowledge it, God is ready to forgive and aid us (1 John 1:9-10).

ATTRIBUTES OF THE HEAVENLY FATHER

Every day we have the opportunity to start anew. One of God's most well-known attributes is His mercy. His Word reminds us that our Heavenly Father is loving and just.

"The steadfast love of the Lord never ceases; his mercies never come to an end; they are new every morning; great is your faithfulness." Lamentations 3:22-23

When I received the first call informing me that my father was very ill in Managua, the first thing I experienced in my heart was guilt, followed by doubt. How could I go see a father I hadn't spoken to in such a long time? I immersed myself in prayer, pleading for God's guidance. At that time, I was practicing conservative Judaism. God is faithful to His Word, and today I see His great mercy towards my father and towards me. God placed the desire to go see him in my heart. I will never forget his face when he saw me and his joyful voice saying to the nurse:

"This is my daughter Claudia, my eldest daughter." "How are you, daddy?" - I responded.

As I write these lines, I get emotional remembering that moment. I am filled with joy because I can see God's love and faithfulness in my life. At that moment, it didn't matter how long we hadn't spoken or if we had been angry with each other; we were happy to see each other and share. I was studying for the law exam at that time, and he asked me about the studies I had completed. After telling him, he said:

"Ah, a student of interdisciplinary careers, you followed my advice." - He smiled and added, -" You resemble my mother a lot when she was your age."

At that moment, the doctor handed me a document to sign; my father saw my handwriting and said: Even your handwriting looks like mine.

My father was happy to have me by his side. He expressed profound gratitude for my visit, and our days gradually became intertwined, spanning several hours of shared time. Our nights at the hospital, filled with unique experiences, could easily fill the pages of numerous books.

Amidst one of our late-night conversations, my father revealed that his favorite song was "Sukiyaki," a Japanese melody. Though he himself was not of Japanese descent, that anecdote shed light on the origin of my love for languages. My father, a self-taught English speaker, embarked on his language journey armed only with a dictionary, a pencil, and paper. In his era, there were no resources like YouTube or downloadable applications. Undeterred, he took on the challenge of learning English with unwavering determination.

Within the confines of the hospital where my father was receiving care, I bore witness to experiences unlike any I had encountered in American healthcare institutions. I crossed paths with remarkable colleagues who seemed capable of performing near miracles to ensure the welfare of patients and their families. On one occasion, I saw a makeshift wheelchair, ingeniously fashioned from a plastic chair, and I struggled to comprehend what lay before my eyes. However, my father told me:

"Necessity is the mother of invention, daughter."

I witnessed genuine miracles as I walked along the hospital corridors and engaged with a devout Christian family who awaited their mother. Despite their own challenging circumstances, they embraced the opportunity to evangelize, fervently praying for others and generously sharing their food with us.

Throughout life, we inevitably encounter problems, trials, and tribulations. However, we can find solace in the unwavering promises of God.

By understanding His divine attributes, we can have absolute assurance that our Heavenly Father will never forsake us. When I reunited with my father, there was no room for complaints, reproach, or condemnation. In that moment, I believe both my father and I experienced the boundless grace of God.

God is love (1 John 4:8). His love is authentic and untainted, transcending human comprehension. Sometimes we want to comprehend His love in human terms, but it surpasses that, and our understanding is not equipped to fully know God. However, we have promises regarding His love for us.

"But because of his great love for us, God, who is rich in mercy, made us alive with Christ even when we were dead in transgressions." By grace you have been saved!
Ephesians 2:4-5

God is immutable

He does not change. The character of our Father, His essence, and His identity remain steadfast. The same God the Father who has always provided for His people is the one who stands by our side. Our Father, a benevolent king, attentively listens to His children. The Heavenly Father is holy, powerful, merciful, and loving. Through Jesus, we discover the revelation of the Father's true nature and how to cultivate a deep and meaningful relationship with Him.

"The Lord is my rock, my fortress, and my deliverer; my God is my rock, in whom I take refuge, my shield and the horn of my salvation, my stronghold." Psalm 18:2

God is omnipresent

He is always present in every place and at all times. He is not limited by space or time. God is always with us. The Father does not abandon us, He never rejects us, or leaves us alone at any moment or in any place. We can seek our Father with the confidence that He will receive us at all times and in the midst of any situation. One of my favorite promises is found in Isaiah 43:2, which says:

"When you pass through the waters, I will be with you; and when you pass through the rivers, they will not sweep over you. When you walk through the fire, you will not be burned; the flames will not set you ablaze."

God is omnipotent

The Father is almighty, and nothing is impossible for Him. His power is limitless. Even when doubt tries to enter the human heart, we can overcome worries and daily battles by remaining confident that God can transform our situation. The Father cares for His children. God's will is good, and even though we have made mistakes and may question how it is possible for God to transform a defeat into victory, we can rest in the promise that He is omnipotent. It is not our role to question and doubt the power of God, but to trust, for it is faith that activates the power of the Father.

"Whoever dwells in the shelter of the Most High will rest in the shadow of the Almighty." Psalm 91:1

God is omniscient
This is one of the attributes of God that always surprises young people when we talk about God's unlimited knowledge. Our Father knows everything about us, knows the entire universe, and everything about human beings. Nothing can escape God's knowledge.

In my house, I have a painting that says, "God is listening to this conversation," and it serves as a reminder that we must be careful about what we say and what we think because God knows every word before we even utter it. In Psalm 139, the psalmist acknowledges the omniscience of God:

"You discern my going out and my lying down; you are familiar with all my ways. Before a word is on my tongue you, Lord, know it completely. You hem me in behind and before, and you lay your hand upon me. Such knowledge is too wonderful for me, too lofty for me to attain." Psalm 139:3-6

The Heavenly Father is eternal
God has no end, a concept that is sometimes difficult to understand. As human beings, we are accustomed to the finality of things, to measuring time and planning for the short and long term. When Moses had a face-to-face encounter with God, He revealed His name:

"God said to Moses, 'I AM WHO I AM.' And He added, 'This is what you are to say to the Israelites: "I AM has sent me to you." ' God also said to Moses, 'Say to the Israelites, "The LORD, the God of your fathers—the God of Abraham, the God of Isaac, and the God of Jacob—has sent me to you." This is my name forever, the name you shall call me from generation to generation.'" Exodus 3:13-15

God is holy
The holiness of God demonstrates that there is no sin or wickedness in Him. God is not responsible for the evil in this fallen world. He does not have a plan against anyone, nor does He intend for human beings to live in suffering. The holiness of God testifies to His greatness, His majesty, His purity, and perfection. There is no one like the Creator. His holiness makes Him worthy of all praise, honor, and glory. It is wonderful to know that the Father is on our side, that He loves us, protects us, and has sanctified us along with His beloved Son so that we can be with Him, praising Him for all eternity.

"There is no one holy like the LORD; there is no one besides you; there is no Rock like our God." 1 Samuel 2:2

Fatherhood from the beginning
Our Heavenly Father has been present from the beginning, fulfilling His role as a Father. "I was entrusted to you from birth; from my mother's womb you have been my God." Psalm 22:10

He has written a plan for our lives. God is always present in every detail of our daily living. The excitement of receiving the news that a child is on the way is experienced in different ways by both parents. The mother considers and speaks of the baby as if she already has him or her with her, and in reality, she does, because a mother who longs for a child makes room for them in her heart even before knowing if it's a boy or girl, and long before their arrival. She can feel that a life is forming inside her.

The future father also expresses excitement, but in a different way, which often creates some differences; the dad may unintentionally say something like:

"There is still a long time to go, the baby hasn't arrived yet." Which can offend the expectant mother.

Parents who eagerly await the birth of their baby focus on how they can become good parents. Sometimes they wonder if they will be the best father or mother for their child. In Lamaze classes, preparing for childbirth, taught in some hospitals, I saw that when fathers accompany the mothers, they often have many questions, they do their best, and share certain concerns. Some parents, like my husband and I, have experienced losses in the past. The peace and grace of God have accompanied us to overcome fears, anxieties, and worries.

During my last two pregnancies, we faced gestational diabetes. My body required insulin in strong doses. I still keep the pen-shaped devices that I had to carry with me for frequent injections; I don't keep them as a reminder of the disease, but as evidence of the faithfulness of our Heavenly Father in the lives of my children even before they arrived. This condition required a very strict diet; it was torture to wait 30 minutes before being able to eat something after each injection because my work schedule didn't align with the demands of the treatment.

Often, the thought would cross my mind that perhaps something could go wrong. Yet, I would remind myself of the unwavering truth of God and His promises for not only my life but also the lives of my children. Deep within, I held onto the belief that the medications we relied on were His provision, and I recognized my responsibility to do my part in every aspect. Each morning, before the start of the day, I would fervently pray for healing and protection over my precious baby's life. I would speak his name, Mario Gabriel, aloud, and immerse myself in the soothing verses of the book of Psalms.

Every day, I meditated on Psalm 139:16 (ESV):

"Your eyes saw my unformed substance; in your book were written, every one of them, the days that were formed for me, when as yet there was none of them."

With this Psalm, my spirit was strengthened, and the comforting peace of Jesus enveloped me. I am immensely grateful to God for placing love and dedication to our children within my husband's heart even before their arrival. He has always taken the responsibility of fatherhood with utmost seriousness, following the admirable example set by his own father, whom he deeply loves and admires. In turn, his father has embraced me as a daughter.

Mario, my husband, would lovingly prepare snacks, send gentle reminders for medication, accompany me to appointments whenever possible, and during our last pregnancy, we joined together in prayer for our daughter, Genesis. In all these moments, the Lord made it abundantly clear that He is in complete control of every aspect of our lives. I often reflected on the painful experiences of the miscarriages we endured before becoming parents, and in those moments, the Heavenly Father provided profound comfort.

Throughout the years, God has bestowed upon us a deep sense of peace, and we have felt and embraced His boundless love, grace, and mercy. We recognize that there is still much for us to learn, but we hold steadfast trust in God's guidance as we wholeheartedly devote ourselves to loving our children. For nothing is too challenging for the Lord (Jeremiah 32:17). We have placed our precious children into His loving hands, fully aware that His love for them surpasses even our own. With unwavering faith, we pray for each one of them, relying on the unyielding faithfulness of our Heavenly Father.

THE FATHER OF A DAUGHTER

The bond between a father and daughter profoundly shapes her perception of men in the future. If she experiences rejection, abandonment, or mistreatment, the weight of that pain will reside within her heart, compelling her to seek a man who can fill the emotional void left by her father. The actions and behavior of fathers leave an indelible imprint in a special corner of their daughters' hearts.

Our little one can feel that she is greatly loved; she likes princesses, and one of her aunts gave her a dress and a crown for Christmas. She asked me for help in putting them on, and the first thing she said was:

"I want daddy to see me, let's go."

When she stood before her father, he said to her:

"You are a beautiful princess, you are very pretty, my girl."

She was overjoyed and hugged him. This little girl will treasure what she felt in her heart, and he will continue sowing those seeds of love to strengthen her self-esteem. Her dad is making deposits in our daughter's heart, just as he does with the other children.

When a father displays warmth and affection towards his daughters, he becomes their role model. Such positive experiences enable them to recognize and reject abusive partners, reducing the likelihood of entering into harmful relationships. It holds great significance to teach our daughters about the attributes of God. Through this understanding, they grasp their identity as daughters of a sovereign King who listens to their prayers, understands their needs, and deeply cares for their well-being in every aspect of life.

Understanding that my heavenly Father created me according to His divine plan was instrumental in healing my self-esteem. Despite my earthly father initially desiring a male child due to societal influences, I came to realize that God designed me as His daughter, aligned with His perfect will rather than conforming to human expectations.

During my hospital stay, my father expressed that women's rights were not his main concern until he witnessed my passion for education and witnessed the various obstacles women could face in their professional journeys. He acknowledged and advised me, "Never cease pursuing knowledge and fight for your dreams. Be resilient and courageous."

While my father was not flawless, in his final years, God utilized him as a vessel to impart invaluable wisdom until his last breath.

A very important factor in healthy family relationships is the quality of time we share as we get to know each other. Every day, we have the opportunity to love, share, and be present in the lives of the people we love. Low self-esteem in sons and daughters is a consequence of distance, absence, or lack of parental involvement. Healthy family relationships are important for building a healthy self-esteem, which is the way we value ourselves. If this way of valuing ourselves is not appropriate, the following behaviors may arise, which will bring problems to our relationships:

1. Insecurity: Thinking that we are incapable of achieving something. We will have doubts even when we carry out successful actions. But we can do all things through Christ who strengthens us (Philippians 4:13).

2. Undervaluation: We can come to think that we are worthless, that we don't deserve the opportunities that God is presenting before us. But God has good plans for us (Jeremiah 29:11).

3. Guilt: Not everything that happens around us is our fault. There are factors in this fallen world that bring difficult situations that you and I did not cause. Guilt does not come from God. The conviction that we can face challenges, trials, and situations with the help of God comes from our Heavenly Father because there is no condemnation for those who are in Christ (Romans 8:1-2).

4. Negative thoughts: Guard your thoughts carefully. The Bible warns us to protect our minds and hearts. The Word of God for All version tells us, "Above all else, guard your thoughts because they control your life," and the New American Standard Bible version says, "Watch over your heart with all diligence, for from it flow the springs of life" (Proverbs 4:23).

5. Constant worry about the future: This behavior not only appears in low self-esteem but is also largely responsible for high levels of anxiety. But the Bible says, "Don't worry about anything; instead, pray about everything. Tell God what you need, and thank him for all he has done. Then you will experience God's peace, which exceeds anything we can understand. His peace will guard your hearts and minds as you live in Christ" (Philippians 4:6-7 NLT).

6. Trying to please others: This will never be possible with human beings. Our purpose as believers and followers of Jesus is to please God above all. Seeking recognition from God is more important than seeking recognition from humans (John 12:43). Not being concerned about what others think about you is a big indicator of a healthy self-esteem.

7. Depression: It is characterized by a negative view of oneself and the world around us: "Everything is impossible," "I have no purpose," etc. These lies about a person can be confronted with the truth of God and His Word. God knows our struggles and tells us that we can be renewed in the spirit of our minds (Ephesians 4:23). God comforts the depressed (2 Corinthians 7:6). God keeps in perfect peace those who trust and take refuge in Him (Isaiah 26:3). Depression is a condition present in many mental health conditions.

If you have experienced or are experiencing depressive symptoms, I encourage you to seek professional and spiritual help.

It is through the love of our Heavenly Father that we have been rescued from our former way of life. His grace has ensured that we are not left as orphans, but rather, constantly accompanied by his presence, guiding and supporting us.

Showing love to our children goes beyond material possessions; it is about providing emotional support and expressing genuine affection through words like "I love you" and "I am proud of you." True love transcends material wealth. It is a message that has been instilled in us from the very beginning: to love one another (1 John 3:11).

10 WAYS TO TELL OUR CHILDREN THAT WE LOVE THEM

In my interaction with teenagers when we talk about self-esteem, insecurities, depression, or distance that exists between them and their parents, they tell me about the ways they would like to receive love from their parents, and through that, I have learned that we can use the following:

1. **Listen to what they have to say without interrupting, simply listen.** Many times as parents, we want to give advice, instructions, and guidance when in reality, young people want to be heard.

2. **Find out what is popular among youth and surprise them with a small gesture.** On several occasions, I have surprised my children with a simple gift that I saw in a publication, like candies from other countries or a popular and appropriate product. I like to surprise them just as Heavenly Father surprises me. God pays attention to details.

3. **Spend time with our children.** Give them quality time, and show interest in interacting with them according to their ages.

4. **Spend time together in the Word of God.** They can be given the responsibility of reading the devotional or a passage according to their age.

5. **Speak words of affirmation. Our children desperately need to hear them.** This doesn't mean we will shower them with excessive praise. However, when our children work hard and give their best, they need to know that we are proud of them. Abraham Maslow states that it takes nine affirmative comments to outweigh each negative statement that we say to our children.

6. **Establishing and maintaining unshakable self-esteem.** Regardless of what the world may say about them, we must remind them that they are wonderfully made and God has a purpose for their lives.

7. **Paying more attention to their individuality and doing everything possible to let them shine as God designed them to.** Sometimes as parents, we can fall into the trap of communicating in the same way with our children without realizing that each of them may speak a different love language.

8. **Understanding the love language of our children.** I highly recommend the books "The Secret to Loving Teens Effectively" and "The Five Love Languages" by Gary Chapman in counseling sessions with parents.

9. **Family fun and bonding night.** You can organize a night at home to watch a movie, relax together, and disconnect from chores, work, or technology.

10. Praying together. Teaching them to place their trust in Heavenly Father and wait upon Him.

LOVING IS DISCIPLINING

Our earthly parents disciplined us for a few years and did the best they could, but God's discipline is always good for us, so that we may share in His holiness. No discipline is pleasant at the time; On the contrary, it is painful! However, it later produces a peaceful harvest of righteousness for those who have been trained by it (Hebrews 12:10-11 NLT).

Discipline serves as guidance, showing the right path to follow. The Lord's discipline involves correcting actions and teaching righteous living. By providing consequences for misbehavior, we equip our children to navigate life with integrity. If we neglect to discipline them, the world will take on that role. Without proper guidance, they may face correction from external systems such as juvenile or penal institutions. Punishment serves as a consequence for actions that violate the established disciplines of peace and harmony within society. Unaddressed behavior, if left unchecked, can result in future pain.

Disciplining children also involves establishing schedules, fostering routines, teaching punctuality, instilling work ethics, assigning responsibilities at home, and imparting a set of values that will benefit them in the future. As we can see from the aforementioned verse, discipline may not always be well-received in the moment, but it yields positive outcomes for our children. Out of love for them, we take the responsibility to correct and educate them in all aspects of their lives. God has provided us with a manual that offers numerous examples. To effectively practice His teachings on discipline, let us consider the following advice:

"My child, do not reject the discipline of the Lord or be upset when he corrects you. For the Lord corrects those he loves, just as a father corrects a child in whom he delights."
Proverbs 3:11-12 (NLT)

Loving our children also entails disciplining them. It is not harmful for parents to take measures to address their rebellious, disobedient, and fallen nature. Discipline often involves confrontation, warnings, and consequences. God disciplines us out of love, aiming to protect us from the various dangers that surround us. Sometimes, we unknowingly cause pain to ourselves and those we cherish.

As parents, it is our duty to pass on to the next generations the remarkable work that God has done and continues to do in our lives. We must share with our children the depth of His love for us. The Scriptures proclaim God's love, serving as a manual for life. They provide guidance for raising our children and structuring our families, offering instructions so that future generations may come to know Him. Our children cannot truly know a Father who has not been introduced to them, a Father who has prepared extraordinary things for those who love Him.

While we may not fully comprehend the extent of His plans and have yet to witness them, we can be certain of God's attributes. He is a Father who faithfully keeps His promises to His children, and we can find solace in His unwavering faithfulness.

Our aim is to follow the example set by our Heavenly Father, who loves us unconditionally and grants us a fresh start each day. He invites us to leave the past behind and deepen our knowledge of Him through prayer and the study of His Word. The Heavenly Father disciplines us because of His love and establishes healthy boundaries for our own well-being. By emulating the Heavenly Father's model, we can grow, mature, and develop trust, enabling us to offer assistance to others.

"See how very much our Father loves us, for he calls us his children, and that is what we are! But the people who belong to this world don't recognize that we are God's children because they don't know him." 1 John 3:1 (NTV)

CHAPTER 7
HEALING, A GIFT FROM THE FATHER

Inner healing involves the process of addressing past memories, emotional wounds, and painful or traumatic experiences that have left imprints on our souls. These emotional and spiritual afflictions have a negative impact on individuals in their present lives.

This book has been a personal journey of inner healing, a precious gift from my Heavenly Father. God has aided me in uncovering the roots of traumas in my life. While I had previously shared some of my experiences with young people and adults, believing that I had already healed from them, revisiting these stories for this book made me realize that there were areas I still needed to address. Throughout my career as a counselor and mentor in ministry, I have witnessed how people can connect with my story, and God has utilized my testimony, as well as the testimonies of many others, to bring about healing. Our Heavenly Father guides us toward truth and, just as He has done with me, offers forgiveness and calls us to forgive those who have hurt us, whether intentionally or unintentionally. In this chapter, I will delve into the processes of inner healing and share examples of how the Word of God, combined with interventions for mental health, has helped me release burdens at the feet of Christ.

The first step to embark on the journey of healing was to acknowledge that there were truths in my life that I had been unwilling to confront. Among these truths was the realization that when I began walking with Jesus, my identity was deeply rooted in Judaism, a faith I had practiced for over 21 years. The Jewish community became like family to me, embracing and supporting me, while providing invaluable guidance along the way.

Within this community, the women I belonged to shared their culinary secrets, crafting skills, and love for studying the Torah and reflecting on its teachings. Through the various activities we organized at the community center, we fostered a commitment to social work and education. I always found joy in delving into the Word of the Lord, and my teachers recognized and nurtured that passion. Their unwavering support and encouragement were instrumental in study centers. During challenging times, this community of friends rallied around me, teaching me about the one God and helping me let go of many burdens.

Being Jewish held great significance in my life, and through God's grace, I was able to create cherished memories that reside deep in my heart. Throughout my military service in the United States Army, they always accommodated my religious practices. Before deploying to Iraq, while in South Carolina, I had the opportunity to receive the priestly blessing from a volunteer chaplain and Holocaust survivor. Placing his hands upon my head, he imparted these words:

"May the Lord bless you and protect you. May the Lord smile on you and be gracious to you. May the Lord show you his favor and give you his peace".
(Numbers 6:24-26, NTV)

May you be like Sarah, Rebekah, Leah, and Rachel. Never forget that our God goes with you wherever you go.

Shortly thereafter, I was stationed at Fort Hood, Texas, the military base from which we would depart for the Middle East. Regrettably, my family couldn't be present at the airport to bid me farewell, and the weight of uncertainty cast a veil of sadness upon my heart, unsure if I would ever see them again.

Once again, God had orchestrated a meeting with one of His beloved daughters to provide me with the embrace of the Heavenly Father before my departure. Her name was Elizabeth Laird, a devout Christian woman who lovingly hugged and bestowed blessings upon every soldier departing for war at the regional airport in Fort Hood. Among the soldiers, she was affectionately known as "The Hug Lady." Throughout her remarkable ministry, she shared over 500,000 hugs, and I was fortunate enough to receive two of them, as she was also present upon my return from the war. Mrs. Laird's ministry was truly beautiful. For twelve years, despite battling her own fight against cancer, she continued to embrace soldiers with unwavering love. Even as she joined the Lord, she received the fruits of her labor, as numerous soldiers visited her in the hospital to express their gratitude and reciprocate her loving service to both the Lord and our nation. Recognizing her extraordinary dedication, the Army decided to name a room at the airport in her honor, the very room where she bid farewell and welcomed countless soldiers.

God's love and faithfulness have manifested in my life through numerous instances. Reflecting upon all these moments, I recognize that He has always been present, utilizing various individuals to demonstrate His love to me.

"The way of God is perfect. All the Lord's promises prove true. He is a shield for all who look to him for protection." (Psalm 18:30, NTV)

MY ENCOUNTER WITH JESUS

Once I made the decision to follow Jesus, transitioning from being Jewish to being Christian proved to be a challenging process. It felt as though I was betraying dear individuals who had been a tremendous blessing in my life and had played a significant role in preparing me for God's service. The sadness I experienced when considering leaving behind these beloved people, friends, the synagogue, community leadership, and much more weighed heavily on my heart. God, who knows our innermost thoughts and the words we will utter before they are spoken, provided comfort and guidance during a night when I sought to convey this truth to a group of friends. He consoled my heart and illuminated the truth through His Word. It was during my reading time that the Heavenly Father directed me to this verse:

"So Jesus said to the Jews who had believed him, 'If you abide in my word, you are truly my disciples, and you will know the truth, and the truth will set you free.'" (John 8:31-32, RV1960)

By that point, I had already encountered Jesus, yet I found myself in a situation akin to certain characters in the

New Testament who believed in Him but hesitated to leave the Sanhedrin. I was reluctant to depart from the social, religious, and emotional sphere that Judaism represented in my life. I approach my experience with utmost respect, mindful that I have Jewish friends who have respected my decision. Jesus consistently cautioned that those who choose to follow Him would need to make changes in their lives, changes that would not come easily.

Often, when we decide to follow Jesus, we encounter afflictions and trials.

"I have said these things to you, that in me you may have peace. In the world you will have tribulation. But take heart; I have overcome the world." (John 16:33, NTV)

In seeking solace, I took refuge in God. When I read the New Testament and struggled to grasp its meaning, I prayed using what I knew—the Old Testament. Gradually, God opened my eyes, granting me understanding and freeing me from doubt and discouragement. Something extraordinary occurred as I began to see Jesus throughout the Old Testament. With immense joy, I shared with everyone, "It was as if scales fell from my eyes," even though I had yet to read the books of Hebrews and Romans. I started feeling liberated from guilt, the fear of rejection, and the burden of religious obligations. Jesus bestowed upon me a new identity, a profound sense of belonging, and a profound peace within my heart. The journey was far from easy, but God's grace sustained me every step of the way. He enveloped me in a loving community of believers who offered unwavering support and encouragement.

I learned to trust God's timing and His faithfulness. Even when I faced challenges and doubts, I held onto the promises in His Word and found strength in His presence. He was my constant companion, guiding me and revealing His truth to me. And through it all, I discovered the true freedom that comes from knowing and following Jesus.

"Then you will know the truth, and the truth will set you free." John 8:32 (NTV)

The journey of healing began gradually. God determined how His work would start, which continues to this day. I can see that He helped me by using these three initial steps:

- **God revealed the feeling of orphanhood that haunted me**

He helped me see the truth by showing me the changes I needed to make in my priorities. In this first step, He invited me to let go of fears and anxieties, constantly reminding me that He is a loving Father and is always with me. I started accepting His care and discipline. He reminded me that He will continue working in me until the day He decides to call me into His presence.

- **He taught me how beloved I am**

God has always been in my life, in the valleys as well as on the mountains. The teachings of the Master show me every day that I receive His love and grace not by merit but by faith. Jesus is always willing to help me. He taught me to put my trust in Him and to prioritize what God thinks of me, rather than what others may think. This revelation has been liberating because God has used it to heal my self-esteem.

- **God invites me daily to make the decision to believe in Him**

He taught me to face trials with the certainty of His companionship. The joy I can experience knowing that

I am not alone and that I can take refuge in the presence of my Heavenly Father is always available has healed many emotional wounds. It's not easy when there are trials, but it is precisely there that our faith increases. Even in the midst of difficult days, we know that God is on our side.

HEALING FROM REJECTION AND ABANDONMENT

For many years, I walked through life feeling worthless, undeserving of anything, despite having many achievements. I always overprotected the rejected and abandoned girl that I carried within me. I was always ready to defend her. I didn't allow God to take care of me because I didn't know Him as a Father. I had focused on legalistic and intolerable attributes, and perhaps I had the image of Him based on how my parents had been with me. I even thought that God wasn't interested in my day-to-day problems.

I didn't know the loving Heavenly Father that Jesus presents to us; I learned about Him through the gospel preached by Jesus. Sometimes I have shared that many people, not denying their good intentions, tried to evangelize me with an image of a punishing, oppressive, and intolerant God, when deep in my soul, I longed for His love as a loving Father, a protector, merciful, disciplinary, and punishing, but also giving so many opportunities for us to know Him and heal in His presence. I was tired of so much disdain, and it wasn't necessarily that others rejected me, but I perceived it that way because deep within me, there was shame, guilt, and pain.

When I interacted with my peers in school, in the military, and in university, most of them had close-knit and united families with different realities than mine. I had grown up in a family with matriarchal leadership, where mothers had absolute control over the fate of their children without considering the opinions or recommendations of the fathers. For four generations before my own, the presence and involvement of men were mostly absent.

And as I matured, I began to understand that the cause was all those generational wounds that had seized the future of each woman in my family. They were mostly rejected, abandoned, hurt, abused, and emotionally shattered, without a promising future, without peace or hope, living with masks of rejection and carrying the burdens of their past, but in the midst of this brokenness, God's healing power began to manifest. He showed me that He is a Father who breaks generational chains, who restores and rebuilds. He revealed His desire to heal the wounds and restore the identity of His daughters. He led me on a journey of discovering my true worth and value, not based on my family background or past experiences, but on His unconditional love and grace.

Through His Word, prayer, and the support of a loving community, I began to experience healing from the rejection and abandonment that had plagued my soul. I learned to surrender my pain and insecurities to God, trusting Him to bring restoration and wholeness. It was a process of embracing His love and forgiveness, both for myself and for those who had hurt me.

God's healing has been transformative. He has turned my brokenness into a testimony of His power and redemption. I no longer define myself by the wounds of the past but by the hope and freedom found in Christ. I am grateful for His continuous work in my life, healing and renewing me from the inside out.

As I continue on this journey, I am reminded that God's healing is not just for me but for others who have experienced similar pain and brokenness. I am committed to sharing His love, grace, and healing with those who are hurting, pointing them to the ultimate source of restoration—our Heavenly Father. (But God's healing touch has gradually dismantled those walls and restored my sense of worth and value. He reminded me that I am His precious daughter, chosen and loved. His acceptance and unconditional love have healed the deep wounds of rejection and abandonment. I have learned to find my identity and security in Him, not in the opinions or validation of others. God's love has become the foundation of my self-worth, and I no longer seek approval from the world.) and the armor of self-protection. Putting on the armor of Christ in our lives has been key to my healing process.

"Finally, be strong in the Lord and in his mighty power. Put on the full armor of God, so that you can take your stand against the devil's schemes. For our struggle is not against flesh and blood, but against the rulers, against the authorities, against the powers of this dark world and against the spiritual forces of evil in the heavenly realms. Therefore, put on the full armor of God, so that when the day of evil comes, you may be able to stand your ground, and after you have done everything, to stand." Ephesians 6:10-13 (NIV)

Discovering that my battle was never against people, but against the darkness that ensnares those who are unfamiliar with God's love was truly liberating. It was equally liberating to realize that many, like myself, behave the way they do due to their own unresolved struggles and circumstances, as they too have been shaped by various traumas since childhood. Before my maternal grandmother passed away, she surrendered her life to Christ, and later, my courageous sister became a catalyst for change in our family's history of traumas, conflicts, and divisions.

Despite facing considerable rejection for being the first devoted and unwavering Christian in our midst, she began interceding for each of us. This intercession endured for years, and in God's unfailing faithfulness, He chose to rescue us with His truth. As mothers and daughters, we have come to acknowledge the areas that require healing. We have fostered open communication on sensitive subjects and established healthy boundaries to nurture our relationship.

The process of healing and restoration remains ongoing, necessitating our continual reliance on God's strength and protection. Donning the armor of God equips us to confront spiritual battles and resist temptations that come our way. It serves as a reminder that our struggle is not against individuals but against the forces of darkness. Armed with this knowledge, we are empowered to stand firm in our faith, thwart the enemy's assaults, and bask in the victory and freedom that Christ has already secured for us.

As we traverse this journey of healing, we extend compassion and understanding to others who may be grappling with their own afflictions and pain. We recognize that they, too, may be contending with inner demons and wounds. In turn, we offer them the same love and grace that God has bestowed upon us, pointing them towards the ultimate source of healing and restoration.

Amidst our own healing process, we draw strength, courage, and hope from the assurance that God is with us, fighting on our behalf. We place our trust in His transformative power, knowing that He can break generational patterns, bring beauty from ashes, and help us transcend the anguish of rejection and abandonment. Through Him, we can embrace our true identity as cherished children of God.

Our relationship as mother, sister, and daughter is not flawless, but it is liberating to understand that the One who initiated this work within us will bring it to completion (Philippians 1:6). Only God possesses the ability to heal us once we recognize our ailments, choose to immerse ourselves in His love, and clothe ourselves in His armor to confront the daily struggles we may encounter.

HEALING FROM ANXIETY

In this stage of transformation, I have come to understand that past disturbances will attempt to sow seeds of bitterness and traumatic thoughts in our minds. It is crucial to seek God's revelation by immersing ourselves in His Word to renew our minds. One of the mental health conditions that plagued me for numerous years was anxiety. When I commenced writing this book, I fervently prayed to the Lord, asking Him to unveil how anxiety had gripped my life. In His infinite grace, the Heavenly Father answered my plea. A few days later, vivid memories from my childhood started resurfacing—beginning with the early separation from my mother just days after my birth, followed by a series of uncontrollable circumstances that fueled my profound anxiety, which haunted me for an extended period.

During my childhood, whenever I was with my maternal grandmother, anxiety would stealthily creep up on me each time I anticipated the excessive and at times violent punishments for my mischievous acts. I knew those punishments would be anything but mild, and fear would swiftly seize me. If I returned home with a low grade or made a mistake, the telltale symptoms of anxiety—constant sweating, stomach pain, and the like—would ensue. My mind internalized these sensations as danger signals, associated with uncomfortable situations and nervousness.

The same held true when I felt ill at ease in the presence of unfamiliar individuals or faced perilous circumstances during my service in the Iraq war.

I have learned through counseling practice that many people are not walking through life trying to be perfect; perhaps they are trying to avoid punishment, experiencing fears, avoiding ridicule, rejection, and sometimes even avoiding being seen. Anxiety can give rise to social anxiety, fear, and high levels of stress.

Having the peace of God does not mean that moments of anxiety will disappear. I have learned that when I surrender control to God over what I am feeling, He helps me cope because His power is made perfect in my weakness. By affirming His Word, I feel that God strengthens, comforts, and guides me to transform anxious thoughts. Every time anxiety tries to knock on my door, I decide to pause and seek moments alone with God to receive the peace of Jesus. One of my favorite verses for affirming the Lord's Word is the following:

"Give all your worries and cares to God, for he cares about you." 1 Peter 5:7 (NLT)

When we take care to guard our thoughts and surrender them to God, He promises to fill us with a peace that surpasses all understanding because it transcends this anxious and ever-changing world. God's peace does not change. In that peace, we can understand that through prayer, we have the ability to resist being drawn into the addictive cycle of worries and fearful or anxious thoughts.

FORGIVING OUR PARENTS

Forgiveness can be a challenging decision to make, but it is necessary for the healing of our hearts and minds. Through my counseling sessions, I have witnessed the liberating power of forgiveness. Both men and women, as well as young people, carry deep wounds caused by their parents' actions or inactions.

It is essential to recognize that forgiveness does not condone or excuse hurtful behavior; rather, it releases us from the bondage of resentment and bitterness. As we embark on the journey of forgiving our parents, we set ourselves on a path of healing and restoration.

Forgiveness is not a one-time event; it is a process that requires a willingness to let go of years' worth of pain, anger, and unmet expectations. It entails extending grace and understanding, acknowledging our own imperfections, and seeking God's guidance and strength to navigate this challenging path. By forgiving our parents, we grant ourselves the freedom from the weight of the past and open doors to healthier relationships. It is a courageous step towards healing, and with the love and grace of God, we can find the strength to forgive and experience transformation.

It is important to note that forgiveness does not necessarily require physical presence in front of the person who hurt us. You do not have to seek out individuals if it puts your well-being at risk or if there is a threat of physical or verbal violence. The decision to forgive can be made in the privacy of your room, in the presence of the Heavenly Father who sees the willingness of your heart. I am certain that He will help you release that burden, just as He has done for me and countless others.

Forgiveness holds the power to transform both people and situations. The Bible teaches us about forgiveness and provides examples of how God desires us to forgive. By immersing ourselves in God's love and mercy, we can live lives free from resentment, pain, and bitterness. Our hearts will become more receptive to forgiveness, resembling that of our Heavenly Father, and it will enable us to listen more readily to His voice.

"Do not judge, and you will not be judged; do not condemn, and you will not be condemned. Forgive, and you will be forgiven." Luke 6:37 (NKJV)

Forgiveness is essential for healing. We cannot honor our parents if we do not forgive them. Forgiving that father who, despite having the ability to love you, chose not to; who, despite being close to you, never gave you a hug; who you never heard say, "I am proud of you"; or who, having the opportunity to spend time with you, chose not to. Perhaps forgiving parents who, instead of protecting you, were the ones who mistreated you in multiple ways. Forgiving all of that and much more is not easy, but if you choose to fill yourself with God's love, it is possible.

Remember that the world may not understand how you have decided to forgive someone who hurt you because those who do not know God will hardly accept how He operates in our lives.

Whether it is a father bound by the chains of addiction, one who abandoned his family, another who abused his children, or simply a father who chose emotional harm, the Heavenly Father longs to carry these burdens from us so that we may experience freedom and receive His blessings. God knows the pain that an earthly father can inflict in our hearts. He witnessed the brokenness in my heart and the pain of my soul; He knew what I was longing for even before I had discovered it: the love of a Father. I discovered that love when I made the conscious decision to focus on His truth and release the weight of my burdens.

I chose to forgive my parents because with God's help, I have been able to understand that both of them gave what they had to give me. Just like me, they were also seeking the love of their own parents in human beings; my parents did not know God.

I chose not to pass judgment on their mistakes but to view their decisions with mercy.

Instead of dwelling on what they did not do, I made the conscious decision to focus on what God accomplished in my life.

As part of the forgiveness process, God brought forth positive memories that foster trust, memories that somehow demonstrate that we were loved and cared for. During my healing journey, cherished childhood memories resurfaced in my mind. I recalled the visits from my mother when I resided with my grandmother. We would play together, embark on outings, and she would always have to leave while I was asleep because those farewells were incredibly challenging for both of us. On Sundays, my father would take my sister and me out for hamburgers or accompany us on explorations of different towns in our native country, Nicaragua.

These experiences have allowed me to empathize with children in state custody who are granted supervised visits. Witnessing the joy on these children's faces after spending an afternoon with their father or mother serves as motivation for me to continue working for the well-being of children in my city. My mother always toiled tirelessly, and she made the courageous decision to immigrate to Miami, driven by the determination to provide us with a better life. Through sheer determination and by the grace of God, she succeeded. My father had the opportunity to witness me start a family of my own, and this brought him immense joy during his final days. These moments exemplify the immeasurable love of God. Even when we were unaware of Him, He instilled in the hearts of my parents the desire and ability to create cherished moments, whether together or when they were already separated, that, albeit fleeting, filled my heart with happiness. Now, I am sharing these moments with you. We must refrain from judging our parents, for we too will encounter situations with our children or with those we hold dear.

Perhaps you find yourself in a situation where you have forgiven your father or mother, yet you harbor resentment towards God for a painful circumstance in which you believe He should have intervened. Maybe you need to extend forgiveness to yourself for passing judgment on God. Despite many choosing to direct their anger towards God due to life's circumstances, He extends grace and compassion to them, preserving their physical well-being and granting them a fresh opportunity each day to leave the past behind and start anew in His presence. The absence of forgiveness breeds division between God and people. When your wounds remain unhealed, you inadvertently perpetuate the same hurt inflicted upon you by others, unknowingly causing harm to others as well.

God offers us forgiveness, and oftentimes, we struggle to receive it because we continue to make room for criticism, judgment, complaint, and pride. We become our own harshest critics and may erroneously believe that we have not received God's forgiveness. All that is required is your willingness to partake in the process, and He will guide you towards healing and forgiveness. God observed my wounds and tenderly bandaged them, enabling me to embark on a journey towards wholeness in every aspect of my life. He does not reject those with broken hearts; He actively participates in our healing. I have personally identified this truth within my own journey. Jesus, the Ultimate Healer, has always been by my side, placing individuals in my life who have played a role in my healing process. You and I can also become individuals who embrace forgiveness and bring healing to others. We can aid them in attaining the comprehensive healing that God offers, bandaging their wounds and guiding them towards the path that leads to wholeness.

"He heals the brokenhearted and bandages their wounds." Psalm 147:3 (NLT)

FORGIVENESS HEALS US FROM TOXICITY

We have all witnessed individuals attempting to unload their toxicity onto others, both on social media and in real life. Perhaps you have encountered someone like this in your own life. In my experience working with young people, I have seen the detrimental impact of toxic individuals in their immediate environment and at school. They endure a toxic atmosphere of verbal abuse, even if both parents are present. Those who engage in abusive and degrading behavior with their words draw others into their emotional state, such as anger.

At times, you may find yourself in a conversation where you unintentionally end up behaving in a similar manner. It can happen that, during an attempt to clarify a situation, the other person avoids genuine dialogue and instead hides behind an emotion—such as anger or rage—and lashes out with hurtful words. Unwittingly, you may mimic that behavior, leading to a futile discussion.

Once spoken, words cannot easily be retrieved, and the offense is not easily forgotten, as these hurtful words leave emotional scars. As we continue our journey with God, we come to understand the importance of establishing boundaries for what we are willing to tolerate.

However, setting boundaries may not always be well-received, particularly by those accustomed to crossing them. God has been teaching me to trust His guidance and set healthy boundaries in my relationships. Though it is not an easy process, it is necessary for our emotional well-being and growth.

Additionally, He has shown me the value of avoiding arguments and respectfully stepping away from situations that I know will bring conflict, whether for myself, my family, or my marriage. Such actions honor the individuals involved. Sustaining a relationship with God is vital for acquiring the emotional health we need and distancing ourselves from what is detrimental.

While there will always be situations and people who try to drain us emotionally, God can assist us, just as He helped me, in discerning and establishing healthy boundaries with love and respect. This enables us to decide whether to maintain a relationship or distance ourselves from someone. I would like to share a tool that has greatly aided me in practicing forgiveness whenever situations arise. In your phone or devotional journal, you can document the situation, your reaction, present the offense to the Lord, and forgive. For instance:

I received a call from a very upset person who was rejecting a young woman I had selected for a travel opportunity. My decision to support this young woman was based on her discipline, performance, and capabilities in her university studies. However, for the other person, this young woman did not meet the idealized standard in their mind. After I presented my position and they realized that I did not agree with them, they began to complain, almost shouting at me and saying things that deeply bothered me. **I ended the call and pondered why I reacted that way.**

1. I identified why I felt offended and recognized that part of Satan's strategies to affect relationships is to generate offenses, divisions, insults, and discussions that resemble wounds you are working on or have already worked on. We can control ourselves and not yield to the first provocation. This person thought they were being assertive and honest, but their way of saying these things triggered emotional triggers in me that were very similar to what I had heard at home: "You can't do anything right," "My leadership style is much better than yours," "I can reject this young woman because I don't accept her, you disappoint me."

2. I realized that I was grappling with a heightened sense of control, confronted by someone who was crossing established boundaries of behavior. Their admonishing tone did nothing to assist me, and the way they spoke evoked memories of past exchanges with my mother, ultimately igniting my anger.

3. When I presented it to God in prayer, I asked for forgiveness for not controlling myself. He showed me that my annoyance had a reason: the injustice towards the young woman. I learned that I can rest in God's justice. I committed to working on self-control and establishing boundaries at work and maintaining them. If anyone tries to cross them, it is my responsibility to uphold them. He showed me that forgiveness does not mean we won't react; it means we choose to forgive and not allow bitterness to take root in our hearts. I asked for forgiveness and also forgave the person who offended me.

The young woman chosen performed admirably in the assigned task. Although I never received an apology from the person who contacted me, it served as a valuable lesson that God can utilize uncomfortable situations to reveal areas in need of improvement: self-control, establishing healthy boundaries, and protecting against emotional reactions triggered by personal or external rejection.

I share this example because when faced with a situation reminiscent of a past experience and we respond with anger or sadness, we may question whether we have truly forgiven.

However, through my own journey, I have come to realize that forgiveness is a daily practice. The moment you recognize being weighed down by emotions, memories, or offenses, it is vital to present them to God and continue the ongoing process of forgiving anyone who may have offended you. By doing so, you can move forward free from bitterness, hatred, resentment, or anger.

On the contrary, be kind to one another, tender-hearted, forgiving one another, just as God in Christ forgave you.
Ephesians 4:32 (NTV)

HONORING AND HEALTHY BOUNDARIES

In the case of our parents, the commandment is that we should honor and love them, understanding that they often repeat learned patterns of behavior that can be challenging to break. Prayer plays a significant role in interceding for our parents. If forgiving them proves difficult, as it did for me, it becomes essential to surrender our emotions to God and work towards fostering healthy relationships.

Words hold the power to inflict deep wounds and hurt the hearts of many. There have been moments when we failed to think before speaking, causing harm instead of providing encouragement and strength to our loved ones. It is crucial for us to exercise wisdom and prudence in the words we choose to express. One of the initial observations I made upon beginning my journey with Jesus was the world's tendency to mock Him, display contempt, pass judgment, and create various challenging circumstances. Regarding these situations, Jesus expresses the following:

"Blessed are you when people insult you, persecute you, and falsely say all kinds of evil against you because of me." Matthew 5:11

Often, when people discover that you are a Christian, you come under scrutiny. Whether consciously or unconsciously, those who place you in that position know that you represent Jesus. Some may intentionally seek anger or confrontation in your home, workplace, or close relationships just to single you out. However, do not let this discourage you. Continue to do your best and surrender control of each day to God. Before the day ends, seek forgiveness and forgive those who have offended you. Remember, there is no healing without forgiveness, and we cannot receive forgiveness without extending it to others. God has made this clear, and Jesus diligently taught it in various passages of the Bible.

Sometimes, the only way for others to understand that we have set boundaries we are unwilling to compromise is by creating a clear distinction between both parties until the other person decides to change their behavior. This situation often arises in relationships with our parents. Establishing boundaries is not dishonoring; it is a means to safeguard ourselves and maintain healthy relationships. While honoring our parents, we must also prioritize our own well-being and emotional health.

When modifying or establishing boundaries, resistance may arise, and it is easy to mistakenly believe that setting limits with our parents is unacceptable. We must exercise prudence and wait to witness the fruits of repentance (Luke 3:8). Often, in the pursuit of forgiveness, we rush to restore relationships only to realize that the person continues to exhibit the same behaviors. At times, God permits emotional and physical distance for a period, allowing both parties to heal. During this time, we can pray, rely on God's timing, and trust that we can honor our parents while patiently awaiting transformative growth.

HONORING OUR PARENTS IN THE PROCESS OF INNER HEALING:

- We honor them by surrendering resentments, guilt, and bitterness to God.
- We honor them by respecting them and not speaking ill of them.
- We honor them by forgiving and loving them from a distance if they haven't healed yet. Reconciliation is not always physical.
- We love them and start anew by inviting them to heal, just as God heals us.
- We honor them by praying for them and blessing them.
- We honor them by helping them see Jesus and what our Heavenly Father has done in our lives.

- We honor them by breaking the cycle of emotional and physical abuse, ensuring it does not continue with our children.

To achieve inner healing, both for our parents and ourselves, we must acknowledge the pain. Once we recognize it, let us fearlessly guide our children and family toward understanding it.

I firmly believe that there are no substitutes for healing our hearts; the only path to healing is through Jesus. It is crucial to understand that our Heavenly Father's will is to heal us from emotional pain so that we can lead fulfilling lives and extend help to others. Many of the parents who have hurt us were simply repeating what they themselves endured and learned from their own parents.

Gratitude to God for the healing we seek is a profound acknowledgment of His infinite and restorative power. Surrendering every emotional and physical pain to Him is crucial in the healing process. Accepting His intervention may be difficult for some. If pride fills our hearts, we may erroneously believe that we can handle everything ourselves or that we do not require His assistance. Do not let doubt infiltrate your heart. If you are going through a process that involves physical pain, remember that the love, healing, and protection of our Heavenly Father are available to all who seek Him, regardless of the pain, situation, or process. Surrendering is not a sign of weakness; on the contrary, it courageously recognizes the need to entrust our burdens to God in order to receive the promises of healing He has given us in His Word. Jesus desires and is capable of healing us:

"Wherever he went—in villages, cities, or the countryside—they brought the sick out to the marketplaces. They begged him to let the sick touch at least the fringe of his robe, and all who touched him were healed."
(Mark 6:56, NTV)

Our Heavenly Father has not abandoned us as orphans:

"You will live because I live. I will not leave you as orphans; I will come to you." (John 14:18-19)

It is incredibly comforting to know that Jesus has not left us as orphans; instead, He has bestowed upon us the Holy Spirit to guide, instruct, and heal us. The Holy Spirit will break the chains of abuse, detoxify us from the roots of bitterness, and fill us with the truth of God, leading us towards the healing we need. Furthermore, the Holy Spirit aids us in our weaknesses. For instance, when we are uncertain about what to pray for, the Spirit intercedes for us through wordless groans (Romans 8:26).

An essential part of our healing journey is confronting our problems. We cannot continue to ignore them and pretend they do not exist, as this will only worsen matters in the long run. We must acknowledge our problems and allow Jesus Christ to take control of every aspect of our lives. Our Heavenly Father has revealed Himself to us so that we may experience life, peace, and hope. Only by surrendering our burdens can we find healing, love, fulfillment, and joy. Through prayer and the Word of God, I have developed a friendship with the Holy Spirit.

I understand that there are various doctrinal differences concerning His role, but He remains a faithful friend who walks with me, knowing every aspect of my being, and chooses to accompany me on my transformative journey without judgment or condemnation.

I am convinced that He will be with me until Christ returns, and together we will return to our Heavenly Father's house. He is a kind Father who has showered blessings upon us throughout our lives. While we reside in this world, God has many gifts for His children. I have personally chosen to accept His gift of peace.

For a long time, I sought happiness in human relationships, but it eluded me because placing my hope in fallible beings was futile. Although I could experience happiness for a while, it wouldn't last because we all fail. However, the peace of Christ is eternal, and we can experience it in our lives. It is essential to let go of the "could have," "should have," and "would have," as dwelling on the past and feeling like victims will not rejuvenate our strength.

Pondering what could have been in different circumstances will not provide us with the assistance we need. Instead, it is our Heavenly Father who possesses the power to transform mourning into dancing, sadness into joy, and feelings of rejection and abandonment into a testimony of His unwavering faithfulness. Through Christ, I achieved victory and transitioned from a state of orphanhood to finding solace in my Father's house. As a weary and burdened daughter, I discovered rest in our Heavenly Father.

(Matthew 11:28 NTV), Jesus declared, "Come to me, all of you who are weary and carry heavy burdens, and I will give you rest."

EPILOGUE

From Orphan to Daughter Beloved Heavenly Father,
When I was born, I was handed over to plans different from Yours.
Bitterness and pride condemned me.

You are a just Judge, Father!
You place the lonely in families, You keep them in Your hands and You assist the little ones.

You transform them from orphans to children, showing them Your mercy and grace. Under Your shelter, You hide us with love and compassion.

To all the brokenhearted, I knew rejection and abandonment without even knowing my name,
I was rejected and cast aside.

I grew up with fear of men and a deep void in darkness. Until Your intervention came, and a procedure was performed,
a heart transplant.

You placed a new one, removing the stone, and with Your sweet whisper, You said:
"You have already overcome your past, I have given you new life."

I thank You, my Father.
You have never left me!
You sent Your beloved Son to bring me salvation.

Father, You set me free, and here I am to serve You. You conquered my darkness with Your amazing light. I want to bring good news of Your inexhaustible love!

I couldn't understand so much love because I didn't feel loved, As Lea, I was despised and rejected.

I thank You, my Father, for receiving me, for walking with me on cold and empty days. Your mercy, without Christ, is difficult to comprehend. It is by grace and not by merit.

Your Holy Spirit has made it known to me.

Thank You for all You have done and all You have given me, it is You who has fought and defeated the enemy.

In the midst of the war, with dangers and pain, Your Word told me: "I am who I am!" Every time I called upon You, You answered me, and with much love, You comforted me:
"Be at peace, my daughter,
I have sent my angels to guard your ways.

Remember my promise. I have forged your destiny.
It is written!
Not a hair on your head will the enemy touch.
Disarmed and defeated, his time is counted.

Rejection and abandonment are left behind. I want you to know, my daughter:
 I love you, and I forgive you.

" Where is the accuser?
Jesus gave Himself for you on the cross of Calvary. Every guilt and shame is collected. You gave Him your life, and your debt is paid.

He loved you from the beginning without asking for anything in return. There is no priority in your achievements, studies, or financial balance.

Jesus wants your heart!
His Spirit reminds you daily: "My daughter, I long to receive you, but today I want to direct you to what I have prepared; head held high, my warrior, your mission is not finished.

Never forget, my daughter, that with eternal love, I have always loved you."

ABOUT THE AUTHOR

Claudia Galván Gil, originally from Managua, Nicaragua, is a community counselor and mentor. She holds a Master's degree in Social Work from the University of Texas at San Antonio. She obtained dual bachelor's degrees in Sociology and Psychology. As a military veteran, after retiring from her service in the United States Army, she decided to assist veterans and their families in personal development programs, counseling, mentoring, and entrepreneurial ventures. Claudia is actively involved in community outreach and evangelization through Matthew 20, a ministry of biblical teachings. In her ministry work, with the help of her husband, she offers mentorship to high school and university students. She also participates in two radio programs that promote adoption, care for children in state custody, and provide training for parents interested in providing temporary shelter or becoming adoptive parents. Claudia is an active member of the San Antonio Chamber of Commerce in Texas, where she represents students in the areas of education, entrepreneurship, and families. She currently resides in Texas with her husband and their four children.

She is a distinguished member of the Guipil Academy: Write and Publish Your Passion and a leader in the Valuable Woman Community.

For more information and contact, please write to: claudiagalvan@matthew20.org

BIBLIOGRAPHY

chapter 3
1. Diccionario de inglés de Oxford. (2022). Diccionario de ingles Oxford. OED.com; Prensa de la Universidad de Oxford. https://www.oed.com/
2. Sanvictores, T., & Mendez, M. D. (2022, September 18). El estilo de crianza, el efecto en nuestros niños. PubMed; Stat Pearls Publishing. https://www.ncbi.nlm.nih.gov/books/NBK568743/

chapter 5
Bibliografía -APA 7a edición
1. Instituto Nacional de Salud Mental. (2022, 15 de diciembre). NIMH» Inicio. nih.gov. https://www.nimh.nih.gov
2. Erikson, E. H. (1994). Identidad y ciclo de vida. Nueva York Norton.
3. NAMI. (2022). Inicio | NAMI: Alianza Nacional sobre Enfermedades Mentales. Nami.org. https://nami.org/Inicio
4. Pichere, P. (2015). Jerarquía de necesidades de Maslow, los verdaderos fundamentos de la motivación humana (C. Probert, Trans.) [Revisión de la Jerarquía de necesidades de Maslow, los verdaderos fundamentos de la motivación humana].
5. Diccionario de inglés de Oxford. (2022). Diccionario de ingles Oxford. OED.com; Prensa de la Universidad de Oxford.
https://www.oed.com/

6. El Proyecto de Paternidad. Formación Para Profesionales. (Dakota del Norte.). El Proyecto de la Patrnidad. R 2022, de https:// www.thefatherhoodproject.org/training/#organizations-schools

chapter 6

1. Bureau,UC(2020). 2020CensusResults.Census.gov. https://www.census.gov/programs-surveys/decennial-census/ decade/2020/2020-census-results.html

2. Pew Center (n.d.). Padres solteros en los Estados Unidos (números, hechos y tendencias que dan forma al mundo) Pew Research Institute. Retrieved December 2022, from https://www. pewresearch.org/

www.ingramcontent.com/pod-product-compliance
Lightning Source LLC
Chambersburg PA
CBHW071117160426
43196CB00013B/2610